Unfinished
Business

Unfinished Business:

Helping
Adult
Children
Resolve
Their
Past

Charles Sell

MULTNOMAH

Cover designed by Bruce DeRoos

UNFINISHED BUSINESS
© 1989 by Multnomah Press
Printed in the United States of America.

Library of Congress Cataloging-in-Publication Data

Sell, Charles M., 1933-

    Unfinished business: helping adult children resolve their past / Charles Sell.

      p. cm.

    ISBN 0-88070-302-4

    1. Adult children of alcoholics—Mental health. 2. Adult child abuse victims—Mental health. 3. Adjustment (Psychology)
I. Title.

RC569.5.A29S45   1989

616.86'1—dc20   89-12097
                                     CIP

93 94 95 96 97 98 - 10 9 8 7 6

To Kurt and Paul
and the other adult children
in our first campus support groups.

Contents

"I always felt like I was different, that I didn't quite fit, that there was something wrong with me. I didn't know what it was. I didn't know why." This was how Phil[1] described his dilemma. Ron talked of fear: "I have always been an anxious person, often waking in the middle of the night, kept awake by fright." Julie mentioned depression: "I seem to always have this lingering sad feeling." Mark confessed to being viciously critical, often more ruthless toward himself than others. He lived in perpetual dissatisfaction. These are *adult children*, a term recently applied to grown-ups who came from homes where a parent was addicted to alcohol, drugs, work, gambling, or one where a parent abused or grossly neglected them. Their childhood family life is a wasteland littered with hurts and disappointments. The glut of bad memories in their backgrounds makes any search for the few good ones too painful to be worth the effort. When they left home, they left it all behind them. They dealt with the past by forgetting it.

Yet buried in that dismal landscape is a significant part of themselves that they have ignored. What they have become is a product of what they were, and they can't truly understand themselves as adults without searching for what they were as children. Because the stresses of childhood have created the dilemmas of adulthood, new insights into their personal struggles await those who endure the pain of probing the forgotten years. Only facing the past can free them from it. If you need to do this because you are one of the millions of adult children, this book tells you how.

Until a decade ago, counselors focused their concern on the alcoholics, addicts, and abusers, giving some heed to the torment of their families and children. Now, psychologists are forming a picture of the adults who grew up with such parents. Sharon Wegscheider was one of the first to portray typical personality types of adults from alcoholic homes in her 1981 book *Another Chance: Hope and Health for the Alcoholic Family*.[2] Then Claudia Black and Janet Woititz each wrote popular books describing special characteristics of those now called ACoAs (adult children of alcoholics).[3] Further studies of families began to show that the characteristics of an adult child of an alcoholic were much like those of persons who grew up in other types of dysfunctional homes, even those where a parent was addicted to food or was practicing religion in an unhealthy, compulsive way.

My interest in adults from dysfunctional families is recent, though I have been teaching courses on the family for twenty years. This book began the day Kurt stepped into my office two years ago. He had made an appointment with me after hearing me tell one of my classes that my father had been an alcoholic. I had mentioned how difficult it had been for me to be a Christian father, partly because I grew up without an example of one. My remark had startled him. "Never before had I heard a Christian leader refer to his alcoholic family background," he said. "My father, too, was an alcoholic. Have you learned anything that can help me?" In response, I had nothing special to offer him except empathy for what he had gone through. After we shared for an hour he asked, "Could we do this again? Talking has been so helpful." I readily agreed, aware that the talk had somehow also benefited me.

Before we met again, another student, Paul, met with me for the same reason as Kurt. After my session with Paul, the three of us agreed to meet as a group, and through our school newspaper we invited other ACoAs to join us. Five others did, and we met weekly for the rest of the school year.

Our group meetings raised a storm of questions and issues. I tackled the subject of adult children, collecting books and journal articles. Later, I taught a class on alcoholism and the family. I faced objections like, "Why dwell on the bad parts of your childhood family? Think about the good things your parents did for you and the good times you had. Don't blame them for your own weaknesses." I probed these issues: Don't we outgrow our family backgrounds by the time we are adults? Is there positive proof that a dysfunctional family has long-lasting negative impact as some experts were claiming? If so, don't Christians have the power from Christ to forge ahead, free of past enslavements? If not, can we trust the remedies offered to adult children by current writers and speakers? Are there not distinct biblical guidelines for resolving our past?

On sabbatical leave granted by Trinity Evangelical Divinity School, I continued my research. At the same time, I met regularly with our adult children groups on campus and gathered from others written accounts of their struggles with dysfunctional family backgrounds. *Unfinished Business* contains the results of my study and the stories of these Christians.   I am indebted to the many authors who have given me insight on this subject. I owe a lot to the many Christian adult children who have shared their intimate personal struggles with me and have given me permission to share them with you.   My wife, Ginger, also contributed much, not only helping prepare the manuscript, but doing hours of research in the seminary library. Deena Davis edited the book expertly and sensitively. My thanks to them all.

There are other books for adult children. It's the Christian viewpoint that makes this one distinctive. Writing this book has changed my life more than anything since I received Christ as my Savior thirty-eight years ago at age eighteen.   I hope that reading it will change yours.

Charles M. Sell
May 1989

Notes

1. With the exceptions of Kurt and Paul, all names connected with stories and statements of adult children in this book have been changed, along with some details, to protect the privacy of these individuals and their families. I have also obtained their permission to use the stories.

2. Sharon Wegscheider-Cruse, *Another Chance: Hope and Health for the Alcoholic Family* (Palo Alto, Calif.: Science and Behavior Books, 1981).

3. Claudia Black , *It Will Never Happen to Me* (Denver: M.A.C.); Janet Geringer Woititz, *Adult Children of Alcoholics* (Hollywood, Fla.: Health Communications, 1983).

Part One

Recovering the Past

1

Living Now in the Past

S eated on the small commuter plane that bumped its way above the Appalachian mountains, I made a resolution. It wasn't New Year's Day, but it *was* the beginning of a new era for me. I sat beside an older brother, also from the Chicago area. We had rushed to catch this plane after our sister's urgent phone call: "Dad will probably not live long. You had better come while there's still time."

We two grown men sat silently. Was he also trying to prepare himself for the first few seconds in the hospital room? Was he taking cherished memories from his mind's storage, searching them from different angles to rediscover or recapture Dad, and by it also discover himself? Was he rehearsing words he would use to somehow say goodbye?

THE PROBLEM FROM THE PAST

My resolve had been a long time coming. For most of my life I sensed there was something wrong between my father and me. Not really wrong, but absent. I rarely felt close to him. For us the term *kinship* didn't translate into something warm and comfortable. I had felt kinship a few times in my forty-nine years, but the moments were so few that my mind had clutched and stored them as if they were rare coins. Once, riding a streetcar, my dad and I were absorbed in a discussion of an article in the local gossip paper, *The Johnstown Observer*—so absorbed we missed our stop and had to walk back. An *Observer* reporter had seen us together that afternoon; the following week an article in the *Observer* reported how a father and son had been so caught up with the paper, they failed to know where they were. I was proud that we had shared something together and that others had noticed; I felt special. Yet such instances of togetherness are mingled with the memory of an uneasy distance between us. There were the good times at the amusement parks and the circuses, but no sharing of dreams, visions, feelings. There were few moments we could label "personal."

It was the same after I left home. Phone conversations were about the Pittsburgh Pirates or the weather or his latest woodworking project. The deeply significant things never found their way into our conversations. Thankfully, we had learned to end phone calls and visits with "I love you." And I am grateful that I felt loved.

The fact that we had so little closeness was my fault, too. I left home for college and never returned to Johnstown except for occasional visits. I sensed little need to relate to my dad and failed to recognize any reason he might have to relate to me. I phoned once in a while, wrote an occasional letter, exchanged Christmas gifts. What more did a grown child have to do with his father?

Perhaps the gap between us was not merely our own peculiar problem but one typical of the "times" in which we live. There's a shocking awareness taking hold of

American men like me: that we are out of touch with our fathers and that it matters. One of the many researchers dealing with this issue, Harvard professor Samuel Osherson, begins his book *Finding Our Fathers* with one man's statement of the problem: "My father gave me a ride back to the airport yesterday; we were alone together. The whole way there I wanted to talk to him, make some connection with him, hear how he felt about me, talk to him about all that's happened between us. But he hardly said anything to me. We just drove out there in silence."[1]

THE PROBLEM IN THE PRESENT

That "silence" was what my resolution was about. I was determined that I would break through it on this opportunity, possibly my last. I wanted desperately to encounter my father, inner man to inner man.

Strangely, this urgency wasn't for his sake, or even for mine. The real reason had to do with an awareness I had a decade before. For some time I had felt a distance between me and my teenage sons. It seemed so difficult for me to talk to them. Not that I hadn't invested the time: countless games of Monopoly, scores of fishing and overnight camping trips.

When they were small children, I hadn't felt the emotional chasm between us, but attempts to deny the gap or to explain it as something all teens and their parents feel didn't satisfy me. I was envious of the freedom my wife, Ginger, had to interact with them. With her they talked liberally—plopped on the kitchen counter, feet dangling, comfortable. Why was it so different with me? Why did I feel this barrier?

At the time, Ginger didn't agree there was a problem. She reminded me of the good she saw in my relationship with them. Yet in recent conversations with my sons, they have agreed that the wall was there.

How to describe this barrier? No doubt all of us have felt it with someone, sometime. At a certain level conversation gets clogged. It flows haltingly, uneasily punctuated with discomforting quiet and uneasy glances.

The barrier was not outside us or between us. It was inside. With other people at other times, the door of my heart would swing open and there would be liberty for things to come and go. But somehow, with them, the door was shut and the things inside I wanted to let out were trapped; I just couldn't say them. When I tried, I felt so uncomfortable it came out sounding distorted. The frog was in my heart, not my throat.

CONNECTING PAST AND PRESENT

It wasn't until somewhere in my fortieth year that I began to connect the problem with my dad to the problem with my sons. Then I was gripped by an insight born from a sensation deep within me, not from something I had read or heard: *I could get rid of the frog in my heart by building a better relationship with my father.*

When I first made this generational link, I thought it absurd. I was in my forties; surely I had outlived any childhood problems by then. Like Paul, I said, "When I became a man, I put away childish things." Don't all of us do that? In seminary they used to warn us to get our act together before going into ministry with the adage: "As now, so then." Could we turn that around and say "As then, so now"? Could it be that the behaviors and feelings of childhood were deeply forged into our adult selves? As a seminary teacher specializing in family ministry, I sought more intensely for an answer to this question. In the next chapter, I'll share what I discovered.

SOLVING THE PRESENT BY RESOLVING THE PAST

Much later I learned that others were discovering what

I was. Family therapist Murray Bowen had assigned a
group of married graduate students the task of working
at a more healthy relationship between themselves and
their parents at the same time a group of couples were
undergoing counseling to improve their marriages.
Strangely, the couples who were dealing with issues
between themselves and their parents reported more
gains in their marriages than the ones in counseling.
Bowen, along with a host of other family therapists, now
insists we can't just walk away from childhood homes
without sorting out and dealing with the emotional
baggage we have carried with us.

This is all the more startling because most adults I
know felt like I did: Out from under my parent's roof
meant out from under their influence; time spent with
parents may be rewarding, but certainly not
necessary.

That's the way I felt—until the dreaded gap between
my sons and me showed up. Now I knew that I had left
home, but home had not left me. That insight started me
on my "build a bridge to Dad" project. On trips home I
tried to learn more about him, asking questions about his
past, learning about his jobs painting huge signs on
Pittsburgh buildings and performing in vaudeville-type
shows. I don't know if he felt better about us, but I
certainly did. Now I wished I had worked at it harder
and that I had done it more for his sake, too.

THE PAST BECOMES MORE PRESENT

It wasn't until after my father died that I began to
understand more fully the problem between us. That
understanding came a few years ago from reading about
adult children of alcoholics (ACoAs), when these words
hit me with explosive force: "Adult children of alcoholics
have difficulty with intimate relationships."[2]

When he married, my dad was a problem drinker; when I was born, he was an alcoholic. When he was in midlife and I was in college, he admitted his problem and became a recovering alcoholic. What a great tribute to him and to God that he made this midcourse redirection.

Though all my childhood had been dominated by my father's alcoholism, I never assessed its impact on me. When someone gave me a list of traits of adult children of alcoholics, I was shocked as I read them. Almost every word described me.

I judge myself without mercy.

I have difficulty having fun.

I fear criticism and judgment, yet I criticize others.

I constantly seek approval or affirmation.

These, along with other traits on the list, had been lifetime struggles for me.

Personal Struggles

Could alcohol have such a powerful effect on a family? I wasn't certain. After all, my father and mother loved me and showed it. Neither of my parents was violent toward any of us children. In search of answers, I began to read of the discoveries by those who deal with people from troubled homes. They claim that those who come from such families may have special struggles as adults. Many of our unsolved problems of today are the problems of yesterday.[3]

Denying the Connection

At first I had a hard time seeing that I had a lot of unfinished family business. I hadn't been severely beaten or abused. Besides, I told myself: "Life with an alcoholic parent isn't all that bad." Alcoholics can keep their jobs, provide for a family and be quite respectable politicians, doctors, or carpenters.

Many experts claim that the child of an alcoholic suffers severely and the hurt follows him into adulthood. They say this is true for those who come from homes where there was drug abuse; severe conflict between parents; divorce; neglect; physical, verbal, and sexual abuse; where parents, in various ways, reject, terrorize, ignore, isolate, or corrupt their children.[4] Add to this childhood homes where a parent is mentally ill, a workaholic, compulsive gambler, overeater or extremely rigid religiously.[5]

I reacted strongly to what these experts were saying. Wasn't it an attempt to pass the blame for our faults from ourselves to our parents? In an earlier book entitled *Family Ministry* I wrote: "Overemphasizing the influence of parents has led to the indiscriminate heaping of guilt on their heads."[6] The recent avalanche of books about dysfunctional families looked like a renewed attack on parents. While our parents are our major sculptors, other events and persons have chipped away at us to make us what we are today. Accusing them doesn't excuse us.

Another thing bothered me about this dwelling on the past. What counts is now, I thought. We can't change the past, but we can do something about the present. Dwelling on yesterday won't solve the problems of today.

Probably the major reason for my reluctance to trace my intimacy problems to my alcoholic family was that I didn't remember it as being all that bad. But that day on the plane, I knew my childhood home wasn't perfect and that some of its imprint was causing me problems.

In countless conferences and classes I have spoken about how difficult it has been for me to be a Christian father because I didn't have one myself. My dad's not being a Christian had left me without a role model. It was hard to discipline my children, never having been disciplined by my father.

A high school superintendent told me a joke that illustrates my struggle: "Sometimes my teenage daughter will come up to me and ask, `Dad, may I go out tonight?' To answer, I first run through in my mind all the adolescent psychology courses I had in college, then the secondary education courses. Then I sift through the management and supervision courses I had in my Ph.D. program, and I look at her and confidently say: `Go ask your mother.' " It's not easy to put into practice what you read in books and hear in sermons.

I thought the explanation for my struggle was simple: I lacked a role model so I didn't learn how to be a dad. Nothing special about that. With all the talk about "absent fathers," I didn't see my family as being that different. Eventually, I did.

Recently I have begun to see traits in my childhood family that I never saw before. For example, I now see something strange about my trip to the hospital that I didn't see at the time.

When my brother and I walked into the hospital room, the usual awkwardness was there. But it was also clear that Dad was delighted to see my brother and me. We talked about little things. Summoning courage, I began to talk about our past family life, something I rarely did with him or even with my brothers and sister. Now we talked of Kennywood Park and roller coasters, the picnic grounds and other pleasant places and events. Our most intimate moments were on roller coasters or Ferris wheels or around a radio listening to Jack Benny or Fibber McGee and Molly. Suddenly, he spoke about his drinking; it was sort of an apology. I was too startled and unprepared to give much of a reply. This was something we had never discussed—any of us, with anybody. Now, after decades of silence, an eighty-one-year-old man brought the matter up with his sons. Was this his unfinished business? I mumbled something like: "That's okay. It's all right." I wish I could have said more.

I now believe I know why I didn't. Experts tell us the typical alcoholic family has an unspoken rule: "Don't talk," especially about drinking. Before learning this, I never thought it odd that a father and son would never talk about alcohol, even though it was one of the dominant features of their lives. In fact, I never before realized that no one in our family ever talked about my dad's drinking—ever. I now know that this abnormal behavior is normal for alcoholic families. No matter how much alcohol disrupts mealtimes and holidays, or generates anger and fear, it isn't discussed. It's like having an elephant in the living room and no one mentioning that it's there.

SPECIAL CHILDHOOD FAMILY, SPECIAL ADULT CHILD

As my view of my childhood family changed, my view of myself did, too. I started asking myself questions prompted by reading about dysfunctional homes.

Do you feel sad and depressed and wonder why?

Do you get angry and worry you'll lose control, or feel anxious and dread what will happen next?

In a conflict with your wife, does she say: "You're just like your father"?

Is it hard for you to trust your wife?

Personal Recovery

Looking back on the hospital visit with my father, it's clear that I was struggling to answer these questions. After the few sentences about drinking, I asked him: "Do you ever get depressed?" I was struggling to get close to him by talking about how he felt.

"Yes, I do, Chick," my usually lighthearted father said.

"What do you do?"

"I just lie here and talk to Jesus." This was the first time he ever talked about his personal faith. This was the most intimate conversation I had ever had with him.

When I left that room, I was floating. Few times in life have I felt so high. Perhaps Gary Smalley and John Trent are right when they claim that our deepest yearning is for our parents' approval, their "blessing."[7] When my father opened himself up to me, I felt approved and blessed.

It turned out that I would receive more intimate moments with him. He lived two more years. On one visit, we read Scripture together. And most rewarding of all, he led us in prayer, during which he thanked God for me, my family, and our service to God.

Closing this gap with my father didn't magically reduce the one between my sons and me. But it was certainly a large part of what did.

I am now convinced that I have other problems that are linked to my childhood home. These discoveries started when we began several support groups for ACoAs on our seminary campus.

The most alarming thing about families is that they seem to reproduce in kind. Dysfunctional families produce dysfunctional families. There is a powerful cycle at work. Not that every adult child of an alcoholic home becomes an alcoholic. But it's likely that one from such a home will have traits that threaten the welfare of his or her marriage and family. Such a person is not merely faced with building a marriage and family, he or she is faced with breaking a cycle.

Perhaps you don't know if you have a cycle to break. You may be asking some of the same questions I did: Can we be certain that families have that much influence on children? Do they create all that much damage? How can I know my home was dysfunctional? Aren't there emotionally healthy people who come out of terrible families? Don't adults naturally outlive those things? Can we really say that a forty-year-old adult is depressed today because of what happened to her as an eight-year-old child? And what about being "born again"—doesn't that make a difference?

Unfinished Business will help you answer these questions and many more. It is a guidebook for dealing with your present adult problems tied to your childhood family. If you decide your home was less normal than you thought, you'll learn about the attitudes, feelings, and behaviors it may have produced in you. You'll see how these traits might affect you as a spouse or a parent. From available research, I will explain not only what your home may have done to you, but how it did it.

Most of the book contains practical and biblical guidelines for dealing with our problems. Some of these guidelines deal with relating to our parents, whether they are living or dead. And often, at the core, they are spiritual questions: How should we handle the bitterness or anger we feel toward them? Should we forgive them? How can we honor them?

This book is not a substitute for counseling for those who need it. Nor should it replace the support you can get from others who share the same struggles. But it can start you and perhaps take you a long way on a pathway to recovery. One Christian ACoA, who has recently dealt with much of his past, compared the newness and excitement of his discoveries to being "born again." I share his feelings: Never since the year of my conversion to Christ have I had such personal renewal. I still have a lot to learn and to change. But looking at something old is creating something new for me.

The greatest reward came from my oldest son: "Dad, I've been thinking about your childhood and the difficult relationship with your own dad. I want to say thank you—for breaking the cycle." Do you have a cycle to break? Reading the next few chapters should help you know if you do.

Notes

1. Samuel Osherson, *Finding Our Fathers* (New York: The Free Press, 1985), p. 1.

2. Woititz, p. 4.

3. Emily Marlin, *Hope: New Choices and Recovery Strategies for Adult Children of Alcoholics* (New York: Harper & Row, Publishers, 1987), p. xii.

4. James Garbarino, Edna Guttmann, and Janis Wilson Seeley, *The Psychologically Battered Child* (San Francisco: Jossey-Bass, 1986), pp. 22-33.

5. Charles L. Whitfield, *Healing the Child Within: Discovery and Recovery for Adult Children of Dysfunctional Families* (Pompano Beach, Fla.: Health Communications, Inc., 1987), p. 1.

6. Charles Sell, *Family Ministry: The Enrichment of Family Life through the Church* (Grand Rapids: Zondervan Publishing House, 1981), p. 117.

7. Gary Smalley and John Trent, *The Blessing* (New York: Thomas Nelson Publishers, 1986).

2

Going Back
to the Present

T he most crucial question for those of us who know
or suspect that we have had troubled childhoods
is, *How much impact does childhood family life have on
us as adults?*

As I sought an answer, I remembered many people I
had counseled. One was a twenty-two-year-old man
who sat with me on a hill overlooking the mountains
north of Los Angeles. I was the speaker at a church
retreat, and he had asked to talk with me about a
problem. "I don't seem to know what love is," he said.
"When I go out with a girl, I never feel anything." He
didn't lack sexual feelings nor did he have homosexual
tendencies. The issue was love; he wasn't sure he'd ever
felt it.

I asked about his childhood. He had run away from
home when he was seventeen after his father, critical of
his long hair, started pulling it out by the roots while
beating his son's head against the wall. His mother inter-

vened and stopped the violence. His head hadn't been physically damaged, but how could anyone calculate the emotional damage?

In more than one counseling session, a wife has confided that she has no interest in sex, neither wanting nor enjoying it. Their backgrounds almost always consist of tales of divorce, abuse, or neglect:

> "When I was eleven, my parents divorced. I thought it was my fault and that my dad not only left my mother, but also me."

> "When I was little, my dad used to touch me in ways that I didn't want him to."

> "My dad left home when I was seven and I have hardly ever seen him."

Christine Herbruck relates Beth's story:

> *I was making Christmas cookies with my mother. We didn't do a lot of things together, but we did do some, and making Christmas cookies was one of them. . . . Since I was almost five at the time, I was allowed to help her stir and measure for the first time. I can remember how the kitchen smelled, kind of wet and warm and sweet. I felt really good. . . . My mother told me to go and measure out a pint of something. I don't even remember what it was, but I do remember the feeling in the pit of my stomach. I got this horrible feeling. I had no idea what a pint was. I kind of stood there for a minute—it was a very long minute. I knew I was going to ruin everything, that this was the end of our good time. Finally I told her I didn't know which one the pint was. I'll never forget having to say that. She was standing there right in front of me with the rolling pin in one hand, and she picked up the cookie sheet in the other. I just stood there. She hit me first with one and then other and then with both of them at the same*

*time. She yelled and screamed at me—how stupid I was—
how no good I was—how dumb I was—how bad and
useless I was—how ugly and stupid I was. I just stood
there. I was right. I had ruined it. . . . I still get that same
sick feeling every time I don't know something, as if she's
standing over me with a rolling pin and cookie sheet.*[1]

THE CHILD WITHIN

Despite the fact that we are now adults, perhaps for
decades, some counselors maintain that we haven't really
grown up entirely inside. This theory starts by
recognizing that our childhood fears and anxieties were
real: Fear of abandonment was natural for the child of
the conflict-ridden family; anxiety was natural for the
child of the alcoholic. With little notice, the best of times
could become the worst of times, as described by the man
who wrote the following:

*One time we went shopping. Dad dropped us off and was
to pick us up in an hour or so. When the time came he did
not show up. We waited and waited for at least an hour
and a half, maybe two hours. I thought he had been killed
or that maybe he was hurt. When he did show up, Mom
asked if everything was all right. I remember that he did
not answer but just stared straight ahead. His head turned
slowly sideways in an unmistakable movement. He was
blind drunk. Powerless, unable to refuse, we got in for the
ride home and to once again face death. For some reason it
was our responsibility to make sure that he drove straight.
We were on a crowded highway and swerving all over the
road. I was in terror, because I knew we were all going to
die.*

*My world was very unstable. I could never plan
anything, but I always had to be ready for everything. . . .
No one knew about my fears; no one was there to tell me*

everything was alright. My mom could have done it, but she was already overwhelmed with problems. To this day I don't know if this was normal. I never asked.

Hugh Missildine has a theory that the uncomforted inner child of our past continues to exist in us as an adult. This is one of the meanings of the term *adult child*. In many ways, the adult is still a child and many of his emotions and behaviors are remnants from childhood. There is an emotional residue in our memory or subconscious that was created in response to past events. We still feel the reactions even though the events that produced them are gone.[2] To deal adequately with this "inner child" you must admit it is there.

Missildine further claims that we continue to be the parent to the child within us. We do everything we can to control the anxiety, to keep it from breaking out and overcoming us. With our minds we say, *Don't be anxious; there is nothing to be afraid of.* But our feelings say loud and clear that there is. In fact, if the alcoholic or abusive parent is still living, we may still fear the same things we did as children. And past fears, going as far back as your infancy, continue to reinforce today's fears.

Life constantly gives us clues that our childhood is not so far away. The other day I drank some strawberry milk for the first time in decades. The taste immediately recreated some feelings and memories of childhood because it had been my favorite choice of milk for our grade school milk break. As far as I could tell, the feelings that day did not arise from my memories of childhood; they were the exact feelings I felt at childhood—more than forty years ago. If good feelings lie so near the surface of the soul, could the negative ones also be there?

As I looked for scientific proof, I came across reports from counselors who work closely with adults from dysfunctional homes. They have compiled lists of traits of these adults. They claim, for example, that adult children of alcoholics have feelings of hurt, anger, fear, humiliation, sadness, shame, guilt, shyness, being different, confusion, unworthiness, isolation, distrust, anxiety, insecurity and depression.[3] ACoAs often describe themselves as over-responsible, controlling, compulsive, obsessive, workaholic, people pleasers, perfectionists, and procrastinators.

Critics of these findings claim that most adults suffer from the same sorts of problems; some struggle more than others, but we all have our bouts with low self-esteem, perfectionism, procrastination, depression and the like.

Besides, lots of children seem to be "stress-resistant," that is, able to pop out of harsh and even hostile homes to become competent, well-adjusted adults. If some kids survive their family life like walking through a fire uninjured, why can't we all? Is this modern tendency to locate the source of our hangups in our childhood homes merely a senseless fad—a sort of "blame the parents" sport?

Looking for more substantial evidence, my wife and I did an exhaustive search of journals that yielded some valuable finds. Let's start with the studies of children. Respected, careful research does prove that children from the same kinds of families have similar traits. In her doctoral research project, Janet Woititz showed that kids of alcoholic parents have lower self-esteem than those who come from homes where alcohol was not abused.[4]

A summary of more than ten other research projects describes the following traits common to kids from alcoholic homes: poor self-concept; low frustration tolerance; poor academic performance; higher incidence of depression; hyperactivity; emotional and behavioral disorders; sexual confusion and a variety of physical complaints.[5] Usually, children of alcoholics don't look like problem kids in school. But when teachers look closer they find these children don't perform to their best abilities, mainly because of failure to turn in an assignment or show up for class; their school work patterns reflect the upheaval going on in their homes. So we establish that children of alcoholics have some common problems linked to their homes.

The big question is, Do these kids carry these problems into adulthood? Until recently we haven't been quite sure. Now the evidence is quite impressive.

Take, for example, a study of those who grew up in violent homes. A major research project focused on adults who, though not physically abused themselves, watched one parent strike the other. Testing showed they were clearly more anxious than those who came from homes where there was a more satisfying marital relationship. Also, the women who viewed marital violence were more aggressive and depressed than other women.[6]

It's tough to argue with research findings like that, yet there is still the cause-effect problem. Just because "X" trait shows up in a person from "Y" kind of home doesn't absolutely prove "Y" produced "X." We can see the results, but we don't actually observe the connection. Thus, we can't say positively that research proves witnessing abuse in childhood makes adults anxious in adulthood, but it does suggest a link.

So does another research project that dealt with the effect on 181 people who were physically abused in childhood. What happened in their childhood families did affect their own families. Seven out of ten of them mistreated their own children.[7]

Just as the abused tend to become abusers, so do the children of alcoholics tend to become alcoholics. For a number of years we have known that sons of alcoholic fathers have a four times greater likelihood of becoming alcoholics than sons of nonalcoholic fathers.[8] Although some studies show that alcoholism may be passed down in the genes, genetics is not the only influence.[9]

ADULT CHILDREN FROM SIMILAR HOMES HAVE SIMILAR TRAITS

Going a step beyond what some counselors have observed in ACoAs, researchers Black, Bucky and Wilder-Padilla compared 409 adults raised in alcoholic homes with 179 adults raised in nonalcoholic homes by having them fill out a questionnaire. Four major problem areas cropped up—trusting people, handling feelings, being depressed and being over-responsible. The major limitation to their research is that it dealt with what people said about themselves instead of asking others about them or using tests for depression. But the study clearly showed that whenever they are asked, adult children of alcoholics say they are somewhat different from those who grew up in nonalcoholic homes.[10]

The most believable proof of childhood family impact on adults comes from a researcher who studied 129 evangelicals. She compared two groups of adults: those who were children in alcoholic families and those who were not. Instead of merely giving them a questionnaire to fill in, she examined them with a couple of proven tests. Sandra Wilson reports that evangelical ACoAs "appear to be significantly more depressed, guilt-prone, anxious, approval seeking and unable to trust others."[11] They also struggle more with spiritual issues such as trusting God's will and extending forgiveness to others.

BIBLICAL EVIDENCE

The family's impact upon children was recognized in ancient times long before science confirmed it. One of the most popular Old Testament verses tells us of the long-term positive effects of the home: "Train a child in the way he should go, and when he is old he will not turn from it" (Proverbs 22:6). The prophets often said that the parent's faith in God would affect the children (Jeremiah 32:39): ". . . that they will always fear me [God] for their own good and the good of their children after them."

The Bible also points to the negative impact of the home: ". . . a child left to himself disgraces his mother" (Proverbs 29:15). Scripture explains that David, king of Israel, was disgraced by his son Adonijah because of David's early permissiveness (1 Kings 1:6). Israel's prophets often mentioned how one generation imprints another. Ezekiel quoted a popular proverb of his day: "Like mother, like daughter" (Ezekiel 16:44).

But Scripture also speaks of God "punishing the children for the sin of the fathers to the third and fourth generation of those who hate me" (Exodus 20:5, 34:7; Numbers 14:18; Deuteronomy 5:9). While this may appear terribly unjust—that God would punish innocent children for their parents' sin—it doesn't actually mean that. It means that wicked parents will sometimes produce wicked children who will then be punished for their own evil. Scripture distinguishes between the home's influence and the individual's accountability for actions resulting from that influence. Scripture makes it clear that God punishes people only for their own sin. "Fathers shall not be put to death for their children, nor children put to death for their fathers; each is to die for his own sin" (Deuteronomy 24:16).

Belief in the parent's influence—positive or negative—was so strong that the prophets had to caution people from thinking they were unable to break free of it. "In those days people will no longer say, `The fathers have eaten sour grapes, and the children's teeth are set on edge.' Instead, everyone will die for his own sin; whoever eats sour grapes, his own teeth will be set on edge" (Jeremiah 31:29, 30).

Ezekiel emphasizes that a violent son could come from a good family, or a righteous one from a corrupt home (Ezekiel 18:1-25). "The son will not share the guilt of the father, nor will the father share the guilt of the son" (v. 20).

That is the good news: We don't have to be enslaved to our past. The damage may be extensive, but it is not irreparable. When the young man who could not feel love asked me, "Will I always be this way?" I could say with conviction, "No, the hope of the gospel is that God can change us; it may take time, but it can happen."

WHEN THE NEGATIVE IS PRESENT

The apostle Paul spoke of the damage fathers could inflict on their sons by warning: "Fathers, do not exasperate your children," and in another, "Do not embitter your children, or they will become discouraged" (Ephesians 6:4; Colossians 3:21). We know fairly well how this happens. In normal families vulnerable children are provided protection, security, and a degree of stability. In dysfunctional families painful burdens, which they were never meant to bear, are placed on them.

Sometimes the negative force on a child isn't even intentional or apparent to the parents. One mother tells of her shock at finding out years later how her divorce had affected her daughter. She was preparing an article for *Newsweek* and had gleaned some data on the effects of divorce on children. She started her interviews with her own children armed with a list of possible effects. With the separation three years behind them, she took her children to a restaurant to question them, never thinking the notes on her list would apply to her "bright-eyed, seemingly well-adjusted children."

First she asked how they had felt when they first learned of the divorce. "I was very sad," Tapp, the eight-year-old said matter-of-factly. "I was going to say `No, Dad, don't do it,' but I couldn't get my voice out. I was too shocked. I couldn't know why. I remembered once he came home late and you got mad at him, but I really thought you got along just fine. . . . All the fun things we had done flashed right out my mind like when he gave me piggyback rides and when we picked apples and when we'd drive fast down the roller coaster road. . . . All I could think of was the bad times and all the bad times stayed in my mind, like when he got mad at me and when he had to go to the hospital with his back. The bad thoughts just wouldn't go away. My life sort of changed at that moment. Like I used to be always happy and suddenly I was sad."

Across the table, the mother checked her notebook: shock, depression. *My youngest daughter had been going through all this suffering and I didn't even know?* I looked at this child across the table, the chili spreading down her chin, and wondered if I really knew her after all. I pressed on. "What was it like when you went to school the next day?"

"I pretended it was a regular week and that I'd see Dad just like usual," she continued cheerfully. "I just put it out of my mind. I tried not to think about it. But I wouldn't tell anybody that you and Dad had got a separation. Not for ages and ages. I felt embarrassed."

The mother, Linda Franke, again peered at her list and read: denial, shame. Now, in a very small voice, she asked, "You didn't think you were the cause of our breakup, did you?"

"Oh, yes," Tapp said merrily. "In a way I thought I'd made it happen. I thought maybe I'd acted mean to you and that you couldn't put up with me anymore. I felt I was being punished by God for being really bad, so I tried being really good so God would change His mind and let Dad come home. I'm used to it now and it's okay. But sometimes I still wish for Dad to come home."

Staring at her child, Linda Franke thought: *She had opened wounds in me that she had closed in herself. . . . I finished ticking off the checklist: low self-esteem, responsibility for the breakup, a desire to reunite parents. I was struck dumb by my maternal ignorance. How could I have failed to pick up the distress signals she must have been sending out? I could have comforted her, reassured her, at least **listened** to her. And why hadn't she told me all this before?* "Because you never asked," she said with a grin.[12]

Apparently many of us are like that little girl. Without help from others, we fix ourselves. Clumsily, with childish hands, we suture the wounds, often leaving ugly scars or unhealed lesions that split open in later life. All of this "fixing" is an attempt to protect ourselves from the abuses.

One of our seminary students wrote of life with his alcoholic father:

As the drinking increased, negative messages began to appear more often and grow in intensity . . . I was never good enough. When I tried to talk about things in the world, current events, he told me to stop the big talk or said `Don't bug me with that.' When I entered the sixth grade things took a turn for the worse. Dad's drinking took a quantum leap and so did the verbal abuse. . . . The lines he used are burned into my memory: "You're still

wet behind the ears; don't be an a__h___. I hope someone
punches the s___out of you. You think you are big time,
but you're just a little s___. To all of us he would say,
"I've had it with your s___; you can all swing.' "

WHEN THE POSITIVE IS ABSENT

You may be saying what I said to myself when I read
this: I'm thankful my parents never treated me like that.
Yet a home can be dysfunctional in another way—by
what it lacks. Children need certain things from their
parents. Their emotional lives are like their physical.
You can hurt a child's body by feeding it junk food, but
you can also damage it by not feeding it enough. Some
kids are undernourished emotionally.

Nowhere does the Bible systematically list what these
needs are. It's as if they were taken for granted. Yet
scattered here and there are indications. Parents should
teach and discipline their children (Psalm 78:3-7,
Proverbs 19:18). Interestingly, in the Old Testament
parents are never commanded to love their children
(perhaps because it was taken for granted), yet it is
implied: "He who spares the rod hates his son, but he
who loves him is careful to discipline him" (Proverbs
13:24). In the New Testament, mothers are commanded
to love their children. When God compares Himself to an
earthly father or mother, we see a more complete view of
what is expected of parents: show compassion (Psalm
103:13); give correction, delight in one's children
(Proverbs 3:12); be merciful (Luke 6:36); give gifts
(Matthew 7:11); give comfort (Isaiah 66:13). When he
compared himself to a father, the apostle Paul showed us
he believed fathers should encourage and comfort their
children (1 Thessalonians 2:12).

Christian authors Gary Smalley and John Trent claim
home life should bestow on children a `blessing'

comprised of tender touching and words of affection. The blessing bestows a feeling of being highly valued; it offers a child hope for the future and assurance that the parents will always be there to love and support him or her.[13] Smalley and Trent claim to have seen many scarred people from homes that denied them all or some of these gifts of love.

No more convincing evidence of the absence of parental affection exists than that compiled by Rene Spitz. In a South American orphanage, Spitz observed and recorded what happened to ninety-seven children who were deprived of emotional and physical contact with others. Because of a lack of funds, there was not enough staff to adequately care for these children, ages three months to three years old. Nurses changed diapers and fed and bathed the children. But there was little time to hold, cuddle, and talk to them as a mother would. After three months, many of them showed signs of abnormality. Besides a loss of appetite and being unable to sleep well, many of the children lay with a vacant expression in their eyes. After five months, serious deterioration set in. They lay whimpering, with troubled and twisted faces. Often, when a doctor or nurse would pick up an infant, it would scream in terror. Twenty-seven, almost one-third, of the children died the first year, but not from lack of food or health care. They died of a lack of touch and emotional nurture. Because of this, seven more died the second year. Only twenty-one of the ninety-seven survived, most suffering serious psychological damage.[14]

Dysfunctional families may inflict the same kind of damage, not by hostile abuse, but by cruel neglect. Parents who are workaholics, alcoholics, compulsive gamblers and the like sometimes hurt by what they deny their children. In such families the addiction dominates the family system. Instead of the child's needs being central, the parents' needs are.

"In the evening, our major concern was how we were going to be able to get Dad a bottle to keep him quiet," said one ACoA. Another explained: "When Dad came home drunk, my mom and dad fought so much, I couldn't concentrate on my homework." Even when only one parent is the problem drinker, the kids get short shrift because the nondrinker is so emotionally involved with the drinker. Instead of being comforted by his mother, the child has to give comfort. Instead of bothering her about his own fears, he worries about hers.

A family, like any other system, always tries to maintain its stability. When one member introduces an unhealthy element, such as alcohol abuse, the whole system becomes unhealthy in order to maintain its balance. The support system that once supported the person now supports the disease.[15] Dysfunctional families, then, are systems that either viciously injure the child or just as viciously deny the child what was due him.

WHAT IS A NORMAL CHILDHOOD?

Many people who once thought their families were normal are now discovering they were not. What I heard in our ACoA group and read about dysfunctional families forced me to redefine normalcy. Was it normal to watch your father stumble up the porch steps into a screaming battle with your mother, which ended hours later only when he went to bed? Was it normal to cringe in your bedroom listening to an angry father's footsteps, praying he wouldn't stop at your room to pick a fight?

Is it normal for a father to divorce his wife and leave behind an eight-year-old whom he rarely visits and who thinks he left because of her? What about a ten-year-old regularly getting breakfast for his seven-year-old sister and then getting her off to school because Mom is sleeping off a drunk; a thirteen-year-old girl kept up for most of the night by an angry tirade from her father who blames her for all the problems in the family; a boy's father who misses Little League games because he's at the bar; a father who shows his five-year-old son pornographic pictures; a mother who threatens regularly, "Be good or you'll never see me again"; a girl who comes home from school not sure what man her mom will have in bed with her? Is it normal for children to describe their evenings as "walking on eggs," meaning everyone must be careful not to inflame the parent to fits of temper? Is it normal for a child to not talk about feeling sad because he doesn't want to overburden a mother who is either too busy or too troubled?

WHY WE THINK OUR FAMILIES WERE NORMAL

Though it may seem strange, there are reasons why people who come from such homes think of them as normal. For one thing, they grew up thinking they were. Unless our parents admitted their problems and got help, they never thought things were out of line; they also made it clear to everyone that everything was okay.

Children want to protect their parents. Even as adults, those who were sexually abused as children have a hard time admitting that what happened was wrong, covering up with, "Dad was only trying to teach me about sex" or, "If only Mom would have satisfied his sexual needs, it wouldn't have happened." A sense of loyalty plays a part in the cover-up. Reading this book may make you feel guilty. Even admitting the "family secret" only to yourself seems disloyal because you feel like you are betraying your parents or failing to show proper respect and love. But facing the facts is not betraying your family. Truth is the issue, not love or loyalty. Love covers a multitude of sins, but it should not distort them. Our objective is not to find fault, but to find help; and we are not out to accuse and attack our parents, but to understand ourselves better.

How do we protect our parents? By fantasizing about what happened. "It really wasn't so bad," we tell ourselves, especially when we read books and articles that tell of horrible childhoods. We judge them to be the fabrications of angry, rebellious people. However, adult children have the tendency to understate. One adult son of an alcoholic thought his dad was drunk about two or three times a week and rarely on weekends. When he asked his older brother about it, he heard it was worse. "Dad was drunk most every weeknight, and on weekends he drank booze hidden in the basement." Denial is one of the major traits of a dysfunctional family; we covered up then, we cover up now.

How else do we deny what home was like? We bury the memories and feelings like campers bury garbage. Since we can rarely recall events from the first few years of life, we may be unconscious of wounds inflicted then.

Besides absence of memory and a desire to protect our parents, there is another reason why it's tough to admit our homes were dysfunctional: We want to protect ourselves. Admitting our parents were alcoholics, abusive, or neglectful reflects on us, and most of us have a peculiar struggle with self-esteem. Fighting to overcome a bad or shameful image of ourselves, we consider our families as normal as anyone else's. Though we feel different, we don't want to feel *that* different.

Some of us tune out the past because we don't want to admit we may be less than perfect or in need of help. After all, we survived. It's not easy for us to admit we hurt because we think of ourselves as super-strong.

A counselor of ACoAs offers another reason for denying family problems. "Feelings—theirs and others— frighten them. They often report being more numb than feeling. Though they invest a lot of energy in trying to appear cheerful, they live with a great deal of sadness and are often unaware of the deep layers of anger and grief."[16] If we face up to the things we escaped, we have to face those feelings, and above all we fear losing control of our emotions.

More than one of my friends has asked if writing this book has been painful. I've told them that remembering has evoked all sorts of feelings, some of them overflowing in tears. But like the pain of surgery, remembering has healed more than hurt. Pondering what might have been, I've felt sad at times, but recollection has also aroused warm and positive emotions. Numerous times I've blurted out, "Thanks, Mom and Dad, for the good times."

Usually the worst of parents do some things right some of the time. Alcoholic fathers and mothers can sometimes be good companions. Even an abusive mother's angry outbursts can be mingled with warm hugs, and this bittersweet mixture leaves its mark. To admit this, we don't have to overlook the good.

SHOULDN'T CHRISTIANS FORGET THE PAST?

I find still another reason why I, like others, didn't recognize abnormality in my family of origin. At age eighteen, when I became a Christian, I put the past behind me. A favorite verse in the King James Version assured me: "If any man be in Christ, he is a new creature: old things are passed away; behold, all things are become new" (2 Corinthians 5:17). Transfixed on the future I said with the apostle Paul, "Forgetting those things which are behind, . . . I press toward the mark for the prize of the high calling of God in Christ Jesus" (Philippians 3:13-14). Like a butterfly out of a cocoon, I felt I could soar into the future, unhindered by yesterday.

I've found it common for Christians to think that being born again spares them from being plagued by the deficiencies of their childhood. The thought is, *Our Heavenly Father will make up for the abuse or absence of our earthly one. We can be good husbands, fathers, competent persons; all we need to do is trust and obey.* I soon came to realize that Christ did change me the day I met him, but He didn't perfect me.

The King James translation is inadequate; the original does not say, "Behold, all things have become new," but, "Behold, new things have come." Potentially, on the cross, old things have passed away—in Him there is power for a moral life, a loving life, and the character qualities described in Galatians 5:22-23. But the new would not come without doing combat with the old. "The flesh sets its desire against the Spirit, and the Spirit against the flesh; for these are in opposition to one another, so that you may not do the things that you please" (Galatians 5:17, NASB).

The flesh, that part of us that is sinful, is capable of "sexual immorality, impurity and debauchery . . . hatred, discord, jealousy, fits of rage, selfish ambition, dissensions, factions and envy; drunkenness, orgies, and the like" (Galatians 5:19). We are warned not to be too sure of any triumph over sin: "If you think you are standing firm, be careful that you don't fall!" (1 Corinthians 10:12). When it comes to struggles with personal problems, we Christians are not always as different as we think we are.

A couple of Christian researchers recently compared the self-esteem levels of a group of evangelical Christians with a group from the general population. They found that the level of self-esteem was no different for those who were evangelicals. In Christ, in His Word, and in the Christian community we can find the resources we need to face our problems, but having weapons isn't equal to winning the battle.

These old natures of ours, with their weaknesses and tendency to sin, are shaped by our pasts, which explains why we each deal with different issues. Some old natures are easily angered; other Christians rarely get fighting mad. One man said to me, "I control more temper in a day than some Christians do in a lifetime." We each face varying temptations and bear different burdens.

We could wish that God would just remove these hurts and handicaps quickly and miraculously. In a counseling session, a woman admitted she was frustrated and weary over her battle with lack of sexual desire for her husband. "I am commanded to meet his sexual needs, but it is so hard. Why can't God just wave His hand and make me normal?" While admitting that might be possible, I explained that God doesn't usually work that way with problems which lie deeply in our feelings and thoughts. Although a Christian wife is obligated to have sex with her husband, she may have a terrible time doing so. A man finds that when he tries to share his feelings he can't bring himself to do it no matter how many sermons he hears about loving his wife. These Christians aren't instantly changed by faith and prayer.

These "emotional blocks" and personality glitches aren't simply healed or disposed of by prayer. For this reason the apostle Paul urged us to bear one another's burdens. By this he means "restoring" anyone who has fallen into sin. Sometimes our burdens are too great to handle alone. When we share them with others, we are tapping into the recovery process the Holy Spirit has provided.

I know people who have tried to overcome a problem or sin using every spiritual weapon they could muster. Often, after years of battle, they had no victory. Then they came to someone with the words, "I have to share this with someone; I need help." And that was the beginning of their triumph. Our Lord has provided many resources to help us face our problems. Since most of our difficulties consist of reactions we learned in our childhood and have been practicing ever since, they can't be dismissed in a day. If you are impulsive, always blurting out harsh words before you stop and think, you may see quite a few sheets torn from the calendar before your behavior changes.

Sometimes God does miraculously change us. But usually we unlearn these old ways while learning new ways. Just praying for God to make us instantly different is like a student who, without studying the text, asks God to give him a good grade on an exam. God doesn't usually skip the learning process in our growth in Christ. We learn new truths by studying or by listening to a teacher. Even though some of the process is supernatural, God usually uses natural means to change us.

So far you may feel you have little to deal with. I hope that is true. Yet, many times adults don't notice "baggage" from the past because certain inadequacies may not show up until later in life. For example, problems with intimacy may not show up until after marriage or after becoming a parent. I didn't become aware of my communication problem until after my sons had become teenagers.

Often, it takes a crisis to make us aware of what the past has done to us. A man finds himself in a state of "burnout," depressed and tired, unable to make his way to the business he's built and directed for decades. His eyes are suddenly open; he sees what others have seen for years: He is a workaholic and he was probably shaped that way by his childhood. A serious illness, a marriage breakup, a child's bout with drugs can cure this type of blindness, but why wait for a crisis? Let's recognize and overcome our defects before they overcome us.

The data pouring in from studies of adult children will help open your eyes. I have combined that data with insights from our support group and biblical principles. The eight "Resolves" in chapters 3 through 10 summarize our campus group's approach to recovery. The first two Resolves urge us to face with honesty how our homes have shaped our behaviors and emotions. You will see more clearly how troubled your childhood might have been and how much it has affected you. I sincerely hope you do not find yourself in the next two chapters, but if you do, be grateful that there are ways, some of them newly discovered, for resolving your past.

You'll find comfort in knowing that your hang-ups are not unique. I was stunned by how much I was like the other ACoAs in our campus group. Most of us were astonished that we so quickly identified with each other. Our discussions continue to be filled with outbursts of empathy: "I understand; that's where I'm at. I've been there. I feel the same thing." We nod our heads, shed tears, and smile knowingly at one another, sometimes as if we all grew up in the same house. Though all of us are believers, we struggle with similar natures and pasts. Most thrilling of all is that we celebrate similar victories. Hardly a week goes by that someone doesn't report some change for the better with self or with parents.

If you truly need to do so, I hope you will join the thousands of us who are finally dealing with home, bittersweet home.

Notes

1. Christine Comostock Herbruck, *Breaking the Cycle of Child Abuse* (Minneapolis: Winston Press, 1979), p. 42.

2. Hugh Missildine, *Your Inner Child of the Past* (New York: Simon and Schuster, 1963).

3. Marlin, p. xiv.

4. Janet Geringer Woititz, "Self-esteem in Children of Alcoholics" (Ph.D. dissertation, Rutgers University, New Brunswick, New Jersey, 1976).

5. Nancy E. Downing and Margaret E. Walke, "A Psychoeducational Group for Adult Children of Alcoholics," *Journal of Counseling and Development* 65 (April 1987):440.

6. Barbara Forsstrom-Cohen and Alan Rosenbaum, "The Effect of Parental Marital Violence on Young Adults: An Exploratory Investigation," *Journal of Marriage and the Family* (May 1985):467.

7. Byron Egeland, Deborah Jacobvitz, Kathleen Papatola, "Intergenerational Continuity of Abuse," in *Child Abuse and Neglect: Biosocial Dimensions*, ed. Richard J. Gelles and Jane B. Lancaster (New York: Aldine de Gruyter, 1987), p. 270.

8. L. Midanik, "Familial Alcoholism and Problem Drinking in National Drinking Practices Survey," *Addictive Behavior 8* (1983):133-41.

9. Peter Steinglass, *The Alcoholic Family* (New York: Basic Books, Publishers, 1986), pp. 296-98.

10. C. Black, S. Bucky and S. Wilder-Padilla, "The Interpersonal and Emotional Consequences of Being an Adult Child of an Alcoholic," *The International Journal of the Addictions* 21 (2):213-31.

11. Sandra D. Wilson, "A Comparison of Evangelical Christian Adult Children of Alcoholics and Non-alcoholics on Selected Personality and Religious Variables" (Ph.D. dissertation, Union Graduate School of the Union for Experimenting Colleges and Universities, 1988), p. 69.

12. Linda Bird Franke, *Growing Up Divorced* (New York: Linden Press/Simon and Schuster, 1983), pp. 14-16.

13. Gary Smalley and John Trent.

14. Rene Spitz, "Hospitalism: An Inquiry into the Genesis of Psychiatric Conditions of Early Childhood," *Psychoanalytic Study of the Child* I (1946):53-74.

15. Virginia Satir, *Foreword to Co-Dependency*, by Sharon Wegscheider-Cruse (St. Paul, Minn.: Nurturing Networks, Inc., 1984), p. 10.

16. Marlin, p. 18.

Part Two

Resolving the Past

RESOLVE

We will become aware of any problems in our behaviors that are due to our past.

Checking Behavioral Reactions

3

P aul, a thirty-three-year-old Christian man, has recently become aware of and started to repair the personal damage caused by his childhood family life. The jolt of being abandoned by his wife and the challenge of a new marriage drove him to a counselor for help with his personal renewal project.

I asked Paul to write about his struggles. In the following account he describes some of his steps to freedom.

> One evening I experienced an inexplicable feeling of sadness and loneliness while I was packing a sack lunch for school the next day. My first reaction was (as in the past) to rationalize the feeling away. It seemed so silly and unrelated to anything. Instead, I risked expressing my feeling to my wife who was there in the kitchen with me. Rather than the much feared laughter, I received compassion. She hugged me and assured me of her love. Later, my counselor helped me unearth the reason behind

the feeling I had that day. My sadness was tied to certain childhood experiences, and the power they had over me had been the same as that when I was a child. But the context in which I chanced to expose myself (to my wife) caused the feelings to "grow up." That is, I got the positive feedback I needed at the moment, which reduced the abnormal power those feelings had over me. Repressing them at that time would have triggered a slide into depression.

The first step toward any kind of personal growth is to face the truth about ourselves. The apostle James reminds us how we tend to resist this: "Anyone who listens to the word but does not do what it says is like a man who looks at his face in a mirror and, after looking at himself, goes away and immediately forgets what he looks like" (James 1:23).

The second step is to discover how our present problems are linked to our childhood. In the kitchen that day, Paul could find no reason for his emotional dip. The counselor helped him connect that feeling to a childhood reaction. This process isn't much different than removing a spot from a coat. Discovering what it is and how you got it helps you know how to remove it.

Treating the problem is the final step. In Paul's case, getting support from his wife was like taking aspirin for a headache. Until she supported him, his depression lay dormant and unresolved.

WHAT WE ARE AND HOW WE GOT THAT WAY

If adult children think of themselves as sick products of sick families, their recovery is more difficult. This type of thinking prompts them to search for healing remedies for a disease no one can describe. It's better to think of ourselves as people who responded in childish ways—appropriate responses for a child—to the problems our parents threw at us. The problem is that we dragged childhood coping strategies into adulthood, and the tactics that helped then, hurt now.

Paul could have dealt with his sadness by becoming a workaholic. Or he could have immersed himself in service for Christ, not that hard work or service for Christ is wrong; but when done for the wrong reason—to cope with depression or self-hatred—they usually leave us exhausted and frustrated. Some coping strategies, drugs for example, are downright destructive. Instead, he found a way to diffuse the power of his emotion.

To help you identify personal difficulties that may be connected to your past, I will describe traits typical of adult children. Then I will suggest how you got the way you are. Nobody knows for sure how our home life makes us like we are, though there are lots of theories. I'll explain some of them so that you can see which makes sense to you.

You may be thinking, *I'm not like the persons described here.* You may be right. Some children come out of troubled families virtually unscathed, and those who are adversely affected are not always affected in the same way. Said one expert, "Why is it I constantly see adult children of alcoholics who are not adult children of alcoholics?" A number of factors determine the impact a dysfunctional family has on its members: the severity of the problem, gender, which parent had the problem, how old you were when it developed, how much support you received from outside the family, etc.[1]

If you suspect your family was troubled, you'll probably see yourself sketched on these pages. As you read, try to discern what "rings true" to you.

THE SEARCH FOR "NORMAL"

Ever watch TV on a Saturday afternoon and wonder if that was the "normal" thing to be doing? Or say no to someone and question if you did the right thing? Or take a walk with your spouse on a Sunday afternoon and feel guilty, thinking the two of you ought to be doing something more significant?

Everybody does this kind of thing once in a while. Adult children do it a lot. Loaded with self-doubt, they forever question what is normal, particularly in the family context.[2] Said one adult child, "I assumed that most people who woke up in the middle of the night had the same dreadful feeling of impending doom that I had." Wrote another, "Though I knew not every husband and wife screamed at each other like my parents did, I never really thought of it as that weird."

Questions trouble them that others don't even raise. "Is it right for a father to hug his teenage daughter?" "Is it okay to scream at my child?" "Should I be this angry when my three-year-old challenges me?" Soon recognizing their own families were different, they embark on a desperate search for normalcy.

With little trust in their own ideas, they watch others they can imitate. Sometimes television families supply "answers"—the Cleavers, the Brady Bunch, the Cosbys. Often seeing only the good side of other families, adult children remain out of touch with reality, their heads filled with unrealistic expectations.

They listen to sermons and read books to discover norms they can measure themselves by. But books and speeches that only present ideals will further confuse them. They may come to believe that the good Christian wife never gets upset with her husband. When he arrives home unexpectedly late for supper, she showers him with kisses, even though he hadn't phoned to tell her of his delay.

The Christian mother is just as kind. When the kids come in from the rain and redecorate the floor in contemporary mud, she simply prays, "Thank God the little dears can walk." The Christian father is like Dr. Huxtable of "The Cosby Show," who not only has the right words for any situation, but also entertains the entire family.

Like picking violets, these confused adults assemble a beautiful bouquet of ideals—the "oughts" and the "shoulds." Anxious to prevent their own lives and families from being like their childhood, they try harder than others to make things work. They mercilessly judge themselves and other family members when they fail to measure up.

Their stories are typical:

"When I can't be supermom or the kids aren't excited about what they should be excited about, I feel like I've failed and I'm out of control."

"I took a class in seminary on family life. My home was so far from the ideals held out to me that I became a grouchier father instead of a better one."

Overly dependent on what others tell them, they may get unusually upset at those who fail to tell it like it is. Or they direct their anger at the ideals themselves. "I got so angry when reading that Christian book about sex in marriage," said a woman who neither wanted nor enjoyed sex. "If it weren't for what the Bible says, I wouldn't have to try to meet my husband's sexual needs." I explained that even if these writers or the Bible did not make sex a part of marriage, her husband certainly would.

Not Learning by Example

There is a simple yet complex explanation for this obsessive groping for what is normal. In a more normal home, a person learns what works in human relationships—a child who knew how it felt to be hugged knows hugging is okay; a boy who saw a certain amount of arguing between his parents knows that normal homes can tolerate a certain amount of fighting without people getting hurt or feeling grossly ashamed.

In a "normal" family, Mom might lose her cool because her teenage daughter left the dishes in the sink. No harm done; the daughter goes away, muttering, "Boy, was she mad," knowing Mom still loves her. But suppose a daughter grew up in a home where Mom beat her for trivial mistakes. When she becomes a mom, she could be scared to death by a normal display of anger toward her child. An adult child describes the typical confusion:

Growing up in a home that was dominated by conflict, it's difficult to know how much conflict to expect in my own marriage. When my dad drank, my mom and dad fought for the whole evening. When I got married I was determined we would never fight. It took me a long time to realize I was really afraid of conflict and that to be a good husband and parent you have to face it, not run from it. Not really knowing what to expect of myself or others has created a lot of problems for me. I overreact to others' faults, especially my children's, because I have a hard time tolerating faults. Along with massive doses of frustration, I feel guilty much of the time because I'm never sure I'm doing the right thing.

Confusion Illusion

Life in the dysfunctional home varied from slightly mad to extremely bizarre. Since this was the only life the adult child knew, what others would consider bizarre or mad was normal to him. And everyone in the family verified that it was okay. If Dad hit Mom, she might excuse it by saying the bruise wasn't too bad or that he didn't do it too often.

Creating Your Own Fantasy Island

Fantasizing may also account for distorted notions about family life. Faced with unhappy conditions, a child imagines what a family might be like without the problems. Woititz calls this living in a "what if" world.[3] What if my dad wasn't drunk most every evening? What would Christmas be like if Mom and Dad didn't fight over everything? You created a distorted picture of the super-family you would have for yourself someday.

Bless Be the Rules That Bind

Lack of flexibility—rules—holds the dysfunctional family together. Normal families are held together by respect and love for each other; part of the reason they get together is that they enjoy each other. The dysfunctional family may lack that sense of togetherness and enjoyment of one another; they may stay together by rigidly enforcing family rules.

People who grow up in dysfunctional homes see things as black and white.[4] They are afraid of gray areas. Something inside them keeps saying, "Not your way, but the right way," which make it extremely hard to risk being themselves. It's safer to imitate others rather than act out what they judge to be their own best behavior. They feel a sense of urgency for doing and thinking what is right, and often they are stubbornly compulsive about it.

OVERDOERS

Adult children tend to be compulsive about lots of things. Sara Martin describes this trait well: They get into "overs." They overachieve, overeat, overwork, overexercise, and overspend. They develop addictions: to sex, pain, eating, religion, power, money, spending.[5] This tendency to be compulsive may be why ACoAs are at greater risk of becoming alcoholics themselves.[6]

It's hard to imagine how children of alcoholics, who suffered so much from living with an addict, will make others suffer because of their own addiction. Harder still to think why a child who endured the pain of being abused would then abuse his or her own child. One explanation is that dysfunctional families produce addictive personalities. Many experts are broadening the notion of addiction to include people who can't seem to stop doing harmful things to themselves or others, like overeating; overworking; shoplifting; or sexually, physically, and emotionally abusing others. They even include those addicted to masturbation and pornography.[7]

Trapped by Co-dependency

When a behavior is compulsive, it is out of control; when out of control, it dominates the individual's life. As a result, the addict's family life is centered around the abuse.

A family can even be centered around a mother's compulsion to care for her mentally retarded child. A woman from such a home explains, "I can really relate to my friends who grew up in alcoholic homes. Talk about guilt and shame. My sister, who is mentally retarded, lived at home and I never wanted to bring school friends by. . . . My mother took care of her around the clock and my father, brother, and I got very little of her attention. Poor martyred woman, she didn't have any energy left after looking after Ginnie. . . . All of our lives centered around Ginnie's condition."[8]

When life revolves around the addict, workaholic, alcoholic or whatever, the family members lose control to the addict, who has lost control to the addiction. The irony is that the irresponsible, unpredictable addict is in charge of the family. A fight between the parents or an angry outburst by a mentally unbalanced parent can wreak havoc on family plans for a weekend camping trip. A third grader's plans to do homework after school may be shattered by his parents' fighting or the demands of a baby brother he is forced to watch by a drunken mother. The young child never knows what will happen to interfere with his personal or family life. He may have to spend time comforting his mother because Dad was drunk and hit her around, or he may have to clean up the dishes after supper. The nonaddicted parent may fail to shield the child because he or she is consumed by the addicted mate's behavior.

The child soon learns that life is regulated by the condition of the parent: Is he drunk, angry, or sick? Is he or she going to sexually shame me tonight? The response is dependency. One is controlled not for one's good but for the sake of the other. This leads to co-dependency.

Some experts call this condition "learned helplessness" saying that the family unconsciously teaches it to the child from birth. Day by day, the child is made dependent on something or someone beyond himself. Individual needs are fulfilled through something or someone else. This leads to a lack of independent action as the co-dependent focuses most of his time and emotional energy on someone or some activity in lieu of directly taking care of self. This increases the likelihood of compulsive dependent behavior—developing crippling, dependent relationships, overeating, etc.[9] Simply put, the co-dependent gets hooked on things external to himself.

When Inside Is Outside

Dependency is learned in a family where a behavior is rewarded one time and punished the next. Children learn to be dependent on cues from their environment to know how to act. They are often not taught to follow their feelings but rather to follow the actions of another.

While some of this goes on in all families, it is excessive in troubled families. For example, all children learn when not to upset their parents. They learn to avoid trouble; but they still feel free to be themselves, and their parents encourage that freedom. The parent does what is best for the child much of the time.

In a troubled home, the child does what is best for the parent and the family system. "No, you can't have someone sleep over," Mom says, afraid Dad will create a drunken scene. "Be good tonight," says Dad, "so you don't cause another of Mommy's fits." Children "walk on eggs" around the house, afraid they'll set into action some terrible chain of events.

In addicted families there is no learning what is the right behavior because the rules keep changing. Sometimes the child's right behavior doesn't get the desired results. Being a good girl doesn't stop Dad from getting drunk or Mom from getting beaten or the parents from getting divorced. The perceptive child learns to watch the family so that with each changing set of circumstances he will know how to act. When the cues keep changing and the consequences for mistakes are severe, the child becomes dependent on external cues to know what to do. He learns that feeling good can only come from an outside source.

The Wrong Kind of Unselfishness

Something else is going on that helps explain why the adult child gets so externally oriented. The co-dependent never fully develops a sense of self because his needs are sacrificed at the expense of the troubled family member's needs. Instead of doing his homework, the kid is sent to the local bar to get his dad. Instead of being comforted when he is afraid, the child has to help Mom handle her terror of Dad. Or terror of Dad prevents the child from developing. If he is beaten and yelled at for being himself, self doesn't develop.[10]

Sexual and physical abuse is such an intense violation of the person—such an intense outside control—that the growing youth is left with little self-respect or self-concept that is not related to the one who is violating them. This explains why a man or woman who was sexually abused may become sexually loose, even to the point of addiction. A girl, for instance, continues to get a sense of self from the men she sleeps with, as if she would be nothing without them.

This creates a vicious cycle: To defend oneself from the emptiness and pain of being nothing, a person finds a way—eating, drinking, working—to be somebody. The way chosen is usually demeaning or impossible. Compulsive sex doesn't satisfy or make one feel respected, and the workaholic is never really satisfied with self and accomplishments.

When choosing something outside oneself as a condition for having a sense of self, one is dependent upon what cannot be managed or controlled—the laughter of the audience, the cheers of the crowd, the sales reports, the promotions, the winnings. Like food and alcohol, these will never be enough to complete one's sense of dignity and worth. Any addict will answer the question of how much is enough with the words "just a little bit more."

Some adult children are so-called dramaholics, addicted to excitement. One man I know calls himself an "eventaholic." He feels compelled to attend any and every big sporting event he can. To do so, he'll miss work and neglect his family, all the while feeling guilty about what he's doing. I, too, sought relief from the troubles in my home in dramatic, exciting activities. For years my wife and I have recognized my enormous need to be doing something all of the time. Not content to sit, talk, and relax, I feel compelled to create some excitement at home or go out where things are happening. When I had little activity, I had little contentment. It was sometimes difficult for others to live with me; it was often hard to live with myself. Yet, Ginger and I adjusted to my craving for excitement, accepting it as normal to me. After studying the alcoholic family, I now know that it is not normal. This discovery has changed my approach to dealing with it, and the results have amazed me.

Co-dependence crops up in other ways. One member of our group explained how liberating it was to recognize his need to be needed. The church he was attending had not asked him to serve in any significant way, and this troubled him deeply. The extent to which he craved an opportunity to serve and the distress he was feeling made him connect these reactions to his co-dependency. He realized his sense of self was so underdeveloped that he craved their recognition to feel whole. This awareness enabled him to let go of the consuming desire to be validated by them. He could relax and let God have His will in his life. "Everything is permissible for me—but not everything is beneficial . . . I will not be mastered by anything" (1 Corinthians 6:12).

Even God's work can be done compulsively. I have often heard people say that to be happy they must go out and witness or do work in the church. Jesus warned against making work or happiness dependent on service to God. When the disciples gladly reported the results of ministry—"Even the demons submit to us in your name," Jesus replied, "Do not rejoice that the spirits submit to you, but rejoice that your names are written in heaven" (Luke 10:17, 20).

I have battled this co-dependency through years of ministry, unaware of the reason for it. I could possibly trace it to how I compensated for a lack of self-regard by entertaining others. I was a boy soprano and sang often at amateur contests, shows, and school assemblies. My sense of self was located in the audience, which I had to provoke to a positive response. When I did, I felt great about myself; when I didn't, I was depressed. I took this same addiction into my ministry after becoming a Christian. I wanted desperately to preach, teach, and serve for the sake of Christ and others. Yet, this motive for public acclaim has been very powerful, and the insecurity and fluctuations of emotion and sense of well-being attached to it have been difficult to live with.

Perhaps perfectionism is tied to this: We construct impossible external standards to live up to. We are deathly afraid of failure because we think success is what makes us feel good about ourselves. Much of this book is about how we can free ourselves from this co-dependency, but right now our purpose is to see its ugly nature as well as where it comes from.

OVER-RESPONSIBLE OR OVER-REBELLIOUS

A woman who knows well the traits of adult children of alcoholics jokes that if a bomb drops near her she hopes she'll be standing between two of them, because they'll throw their bodies over her. When it comes to responsibility, adult children are extreme: they are either overly responsible or irresponsible. Janet Woititz, the first to write about this, suggests this comes from our attempt to please our parents. "You take it all on or you give it all up. There is no middle ground. You tried to please your parents, doing more and more and more, or you reached the point where you recognized it didn't matter, so you did nothing."[11]

Adult children are often heralded for their great achievements. They are recognized for their dependability and chosen as leaders. But an ultra sense of responsibility is a heavy burden to bear and it may produce false guilt over things unconnected with them. This may be a continuation of feeling responsible for their parents' divorce or drinking or abuse.

Often they are compulsive overachievers, taking on more than they can handle and ending up burned out. They take themselves more seriously than they ought, and criticism is difficult to hear because so much is at stake. How well you do is so closely connected to how well you feel about yourself. This makes it hard to have fun, even when it's deserved and needed.

On the other hand, being irresponsible doesn't make life any easier. Such adult children may not have been encouraged to finish projects and weren't properly rewarded for their accomplishments. Or parents gave so little affirmation, they gave up trying to earn it. They go through life unable to cope with challenges, insensitive to the needs of others and to their own potential.

A Symptom of Co-dependency

Co-dependency produces extreme approaches to responsibility in this way: The dysfunctional family is an emotional survival system whose members are filled with hate and love toward the problem parent. Amidst chaos, confusion, misery, and preoccupation with the unsolvable "problem," each takes a certain role. In turn, the family system rewards and rejects, pressuring its members into roles. In more normal circumstances, this produces good results. But in the alcoholic and abusive home, the process is one of survival, and the techniques or roles chosen by or forced upon the individual are not mere adjustments but maladjustments. The roles make life worse for everyone, the addict as well as family members. When out from under their childhood roof, adult children continue to play the roles because they have become addicted to them.[12]

Through extensive work in treating alcoholic families, Sharon Wegscheider-Cruse has described these roles, although the models she gives us are not the final word. Perhaps families that are not dysfunctional have similar roles, and certainly not everyone in a dysfunctional family entirely fits the description of any of them. Sometimes members change roles or have traits similar to several of them.

Always the Hero

Wegscheider calls the overly responsible person the "hero." "He provides those moments of hope and pride that even the most desperate families experience from time to time, furnishing a source of worth for the family when all other sources have run dry."[13] He or she gets this way by taking up the slack caused by the dysfunctional parent. Often this is the oldest child, who washes clothes, cooks meals and cares for the other children. Or it can be an only child who awakens the alcoholic mother and gets her off to work. Perhaps the hero personality develops from an attempt to please an abusive father or to overcome the shame brought on by sexual abuse. At any rate, it is an attempt to make the family survive and to save the family name or to stop whatever is troubling the family.

It is all in vain, because the problem parent can't be changed by the hero's efforts. No matter what he does, the drinking gets worse. In fact, protecting the parent and family reduces the negative consequences that might make the troubled parent come to his or her senses. All the while, the hero grows into a good, competent, considerate, successful person. He or she has been forced into the parental role because the parents have abandoned theirs. This role reversal causes great insecurity in children; they literally raise themselves.[14]

The boy who confronts his father when he's drinking or tries to cheer his mother because of his father's drinking is like the daughter who is forced to respond to her father's sexual demands. By playing the role the parent is supposed to play, they are denied their childhoods. They have been put into a position of protecting rather than being protected, of supervising rather than being supervised, of disciplining instead of being disciplined. This produces adults who only feel good about themselves when they care for others. Any little favor others do for them is rarely received without feeling guilty. They find it difficult to depend on others for their emotional needs. They may even have difficulty cooperating with others on a work project. They are driven to care for other people, at the expense of caring for themselves.[15]

Heroes can easily take on the role of enablers as adults. Their co-dependency causes them to be attracted to weak, needy persons, and they often end up marrying alcoholics.

The twist to this is that they may get angry at people who make demands on them because their overdeveloped sense of responsibility makes it too difficult to say no. They choose and even create people who need them, all the while resenting that they do.

Ministers and social workers, without realizing what they are doing, often encourage people to continue to overcare. Believing it's possible to overcome evil with good, they counsel the wife of the alcoholic to love and care for him in an effort to make the drinker wake up to his problem. The best way to love a problem drinker is to say no to his or her demands for care. Let him mop up his own vomit, face his financial and other problems, and otherwise reap the fruit of his irresponsible behavior. Social workers and ministers who mistake overcaring for love often are co-dependents themselves. They measure success in terms of the number of troubled people they can help.

Success can never satisfy the overly responsible person's needs nor wipe out the disgrace he or she feels for the family. Yet, the hero continues to play the role without fully realizing he is doing so or why. One member of our group wrote:

> *I came from a family of underachievers, welfare addicts, alcoholics, dropouts. I usually refer to my family affectionately as "low-life scumbags." And I decided at a young age to achieve. I did very well in school and very well in college. I have a management position now and am a very good worker and greatly appreciated by my employers. Before I became a Christian my "success" was my number one motivation, almost to the neglect of my children. Now I am much less serious about achieving. I would gladly be a housewife. Others at work, though, still see me as career-oriented, so perhaps I still have a problem with this. I often don't feel that I'm doing a job as well as I could.*

Cop Out to Cope

The role of scapegoat accounts in part for the number of rebellious kids from troubled homes. Usually someone takes the scapegoat role because another family member has already taken the hero position in the family. When the hero gets praise for helping the situation, the scapegoat gets the blame for making it worse. His efforts to stop parental abuse or addiction are in the form of "flight." Starved for the attention of his parents and trying to cope with the family troubles, the scapegoat fights the bad with bad. In reverse of the hero role, he fights the family problem by becoming a problem. The scapegoat now becomes the one on whom to blame the family troubles, something that helps the family continue to deny the real problem.

A seminary student who suffered severe abuse in the scapegoat role tells how he began acting out the things he was being accused of.

That year my home was like a prison camp. I was subject to surprise searches. My pockets were checked often and at different times. My breath was checked for "pot smell," even though I wasn't doing drugs. In the middle of the night or early morning my father would come into my room and question me about my activities. Once in a while he would loudly accuse me of masturbating. The verbal abuse just kept growing. He accused me of acting feminine. I was a pervert, a queer, a "hot head," a liar and most of all, many times a day he would call me an A__H___. As was the style at the time I had a pony-tail. He would walk behind me and pull my hair and hit me on the head while he called me names. Eventually I did start using drugs. On occasion I did actually get caught getting high. Once this happened during one of his dry times. That night he took out a bottle and started drinking. He made me stay up all night with him making sure I knew that everything was my fault.

It was through a concerned high school counselor and a later conversion to Christ that this man was rescued from an irresponsible lifestyle.

Sometimes a member of a dysfunctional home points the finger at the family problem, and in turn is blamed for the family problems. The family turns against anyone who wants to break down the wall of denial.

One of the women in our group explained how she has been trying to persuade her mother to seek treatment for alcoholism. Neither the mother nor the rest of the family believes there is a problem. She says, "My brothers and sisters are constantly telling me to `get off Mom's back.' They blame me for causing trouble even when I'm not. Just last week my sister phoned me to tell me to stop bothering Mom, yet I hadn't written or phoned my mother for the past six months."

Wegscheider describes several other roles, which we'll look at later in connection with other traits.

INTIMIDATED BY INTIMACY

Adult children have a difficult time with intimate relationships. Whether the problem shows up as an "emotional block," like the one I had with my boys, or as sexual inhibition with a spouse, being unable to be intimate may be part of the way we defended ourselves in a dysfunctional family system.

The "lost child" described by Wegscheider-Cruse learned to shun intimacy.[16] To adapt to a chaotic home life the "lost child" covers up the situation by losing herself in the background, keeping out of everyone's way, finding more comfort in the privacy of her own company than in the midst of the family. A set of false feelings covers up the painful, real feelings, which she tries to deny. She wears a false front for others: "I'm just fine, thank you."

In adulthood, this person may continue to withdraw, expecting little of herself. On the job she may vanish into the woodwork, working harder to avoid being noticed than to being promoted. She, like some other members of dysfunctional homes, may be expert in the art of adapting. As a salesperson, she may try not to sell too much or too little lest her boss raise her quota or lower the boom. The lost child will lose out through lack of relational skills resulting from her habit of covering up.

Cover Up, Clam Up

Because children want to be loyal to their mothers and fathers, they conform to the standard rules "don't feel and don't talk." They don't mention the shame, hurt, and emotional pain each member is suffering. Even when terrorized night after night by an abusive father, a child will not talk to others about how he or she feels. As a result, the dysfunctional family doesn't deal much with feelings. If they did, they would have to face the problem. Their fear of exposing the problem turns into a fear of exposing themselves.

Life in the Dry State

The alcoholic or abuser lives in one of two states: when drugged (or angry) and when sober (or calm). Call them the wet and the dry states for the alcoholic. In the typical alcoholic family the wet state is more exciting for all the family members. There is more interaction and more eye contact. They are much more in touch with their feelings, more alive and intimate. The same may be true for the family of the hot-tempered parent, who has much more intense contact with his child when he is angry than when he is calm. Even when the contact is so hurtful, it may be less painful than having no contact at all. In this case, the parent drinks in order to be intimate, or gets angry in order to get close.

In the dry state, the family has little interaction. Some research suggests that, unconsciously, family members would rather have the alcoholic in a drinking state because life is more interesting. The drugs or the anger serve a purpose. Having a drink allows them to talk and helps them to handle conflict, so they think. It makes them assertive, something they can't seem to be in the dry state. The problem with this, of course, is that the addicted person's attempts at intimacy are clumsy, and his or her effort to be assertive turns into violent, selfish aggression.

SUPER REACTORS

It's common for adult children to overreact, especially to changes they feel they can't control. One ACoA put it clearly. "Whenever one of the kids gives us a little trouble, I get so upset at first that every response I make is wrong. I complain, `Why did this have to happen?' I blame, `What's wrong with this child?' I moan, `What are we going to do now?' My wife, instead, takes it in stride and begins to do something about it." Any kind of crisis or problem can provoke this overreaction from adult children.

Dysfunctional Family Issue Number One: Control

Loss of control for the adult child's family was far more serious than in the average family. If Dad usually gambled away his paycheck, or couldn't work because he was drunk, or regularly canceled family outings because he had to work, the whole family suffered. Instead of safe and predictable, life was threatening and chaotic. To survive, family members had to control as much as possible. As adults, these survivors are so afraid of things being out of control that any little crisis will send them into a panic.

The Like It Or Not Likeness

Research suggests that we behave a lot like our parents; we especially identify and imitate the same sex parent. As role models, they influence us even if we are not conscious of it. We may even adopt some of their behaviors we grossly disliked. "I never saw my alcoholic dad handle a problem," said one ACoA. "My mother always handled things. Whenever there was a crisis, he would come unglued. Though I don't drink, I tend to react the same way as he."

One ACoA believes this may explain the mystery of one of his reactions:

For some reason the basement has become my domain. I criticize and complain to my wife about how the kids go down there and then don't take care of it. I could never understand how she would put up with their irresponsibility. Recently, we were having a talk with my older brother about our home. He mentioned that when my dad came home drunk he would go to the basement and find something wrong. A screwdriver was missing or something was out of place and he would swear and yell about it. He didn't talk or teach; he just reacted. My wife explained that perhaps that is the reason why the basement is such an issue to me.

It's possible that adult children have two sets of reactions. Sometimes they react calmly and generously like Mom did when she had a few drinks or Dad did when he got high on work or food or whatever. At other times they are critical and angry. It's not a substance like alcohol or drugs, but a mood that creates the intense change in their reactions.

Act Now, Think Later

Impulsiveness may contribute to the tendency to overreact. Woititz ties this to the chaotic condition in alcoholic families. Because you weren't sure what would happen in the future, you learned to grab what you could of satisfaction and happiness when it presented itself. If your parents said wait until next week, you couldn't rely on their promises. Because you didn't look forward to happy times with any degree of confidence, you leaned toward instant gratification. Instead of thinking ahead, planning, and sacrificing for the future, you learned to act impulsively. You didn't learn a cool, calculated approach to problem solving; you learned to impulsively overreact.

THE SUM OF IT

Behaviors learned in a dysfunctional home are not all bad. Adult children are terrific caregivers, usually more sensitive to others and ready to sacrifice for them. Yet, they may rarely feel fulfilled or satisfied because they try to do more than their share for people—just as they did in their childhood homes. And they may have some habits that are difficult to change: they overreact, have trouble talking about their feelings, are extremely critical, etc.

Perhaps they behave like they do because they're simply chips off the old block. Or there may be a more complex explanation: They didn't really develop a true self because they were so externally oriented. They keep longing for approval from others—outside cues that they are okay and their actions are all right. Very likely, we adult children became like we are today through our attempts to cope with a difficult situation.

Think of the family as a boat. The dysfunctional family member is always rocking the boat, threatening everyone on board. So if you can't keep the person from shaking the boat, you have to do whatever you can to keep it steady. Family counselors call this homeostasis.

Ask yourself these questions: "When the boat began to rock, what did I do to keep it steady?" "When the boat was rocking, how did I feel?" We'll talk about that last question next.

Notes

1. Robert K. Ackerman, *Same House, Different Homes: Why Adult Children of Alcoholics Are Not All the Same* (Pompano Beach, Fla.: Health Communications, Inc., 1987).

2. Janet Geringer Woititz, *Adult Children of Alcoholics*, p. 24.

3. Ibid., p. 25.

4. Marlin, p. 50.

5. Sara Hines Martin, *Healing for Adult Children of Alcoholics* (Nashville: Broadman Press, 1988), p. 14.

6. Steinglass, p. 295.

7. Merle A. Fossum and Marilyn J. Mason, *Facing Shame: Families in Recovery* (New York: W. W. Norton & Co., 1986), p. 9.

8. Marlin, pp. 5, 6.

9. Patricia O'Gorman and Philip Oliver-Diaz, *Breaking the Cycle of Addition: A Parent's Guide to Raising Healthy Kids* (Pompano Beach, Fla.: Health Communications, Inc., 1987), p. 31.

10. Whitfield, p. 30.

11. Woititz, *Adult Children of Alcoholics*, p. 47.

12. Sharon Wegscheider-Cruse, *Another Chance: Hope and Health for the Alcoholic Family* (Palo Alto, Calif: Science and Behavior Books, 1981), pp. 104-15.

13. Ibid., p. 104.

14. Martin, p. 39.

15. Wegscheider-Cruse, pp.104-15.

16. Ibid., pp. 127-36.

RESOLVE

We will become aware of
present emotional problems
that stem from the past
and own these as our own.

4

Appraising Emotional Harm

O ne of the members of our group, whose father was an alcoholic, related the following:

I can distinctly remember trying to get my mother and dad to stop yelling at each other. When my father came home drunk, my mother always picked a fight with him, even though we kids pleaded with her not to. One evening, when I was seven or eight years old, I was so emotionally upset by their screaming that I sort of lost control of myself and acted crazy. I ran through the living room and up the stairs screaming, "Stop it; stop it; I can't stand it anymore." I can't remember exactly what happened, but I know my parents turned their attention toward me. However, it wasn't to comfort me or to let me talk out my feelings; rather, they told me how foolish and unnecessary my behavior was. Only in my middle-age years have I begun to look more closely at my childhood. It's now clear that I was far more emotionally upset at the time than I ever realized.

*I began to think of the skin rash I had as a child in a
different way. The sores on my chin and the bottom of my
feet didn't respond to numerous ointments prescribed by
our family doctor. After years of scratching myself a
doctor told my mother to have me tape the affected area
with adhesive tape. The irritation went away. Only a few
weeks ago, over forty years later, I found the answer to the
mystery. When I described the condition to my doctor, he
easily diagnosed it as a skin condition caused by stress. I
was literally tearing out sections of skin with my
fingernails. As an adult, I never thought I was that
emotionally disturbed as a child. I am now seeing how my
emotional responses today are tied to those of the past.*

This man has a lot in common with others from
dysfunctional homes who fought tremendous emotional
upheavals as children and now find themselves with
similar struggles as adults. Resolving to identify these
emotions is a major step in dealing with them. Let's
discuss the most frequent emotions adult children talk
about.

MAIMED BY SHAME

*Whenever I go to a social event, I feel like I don't belong,
that somehow I am different. All evening long I fight the
feeling that someone is going to come up to me and say,
"Please leave; you don't belong here." Life is a party you
attend to which you haven't been invited.*

This feeling of shame lies behind the self-esteem
problem so many of us have. We not only dislike
ourselves, we are ashamed of who we are. It drives us to
achieve and traps us in the role of people-pleasers to
prove to ourselves and the world that we have worth.

Low self-esteem may make adults maliciously critical
of others, and may account for their awful fear of
criticism. Lack of self-esteem can account for shyness,

loneliness and depression. People with low self-esteem feel isolated, unlovable, too weak to overcome their deficiencies, and unable to defend themselves. They also fear angering others.

Self-disclosure is extremely difficult because they may feel they have little of self worth disclosing. It can account for why some adult children are habitual liars; they fabricate stories to make themselves or their parents look good. People with a low view of themselves may argue that their family didn't make them feel that way; instead, they remember things that happened in school or on the playground that made them feel terrible about themselves. In most cases, life in the home started them down the road of self-doubt and shame.

We know that low self-esteem in children makes them more anxious about themselves and their relationships to others. When they play with kids in the neighborhood or relate to peers at school, their anxiety makes them do and say things that provoke others to react negatively to them. What started in the home continues outside of it.[1]

Negative Messages or None at All

There are many ways to explain an adult child's poor self-image. It could simply be linked to a lack of affirmation. Perhaps the child never heard, "Boy, you handled that well," or "You are talented." Perhaps a child was frequently criticized: "You should be ashamed of yourself," or "You'll never amount to anything, stupid." Such statements are etched on adult brains, and no doubt are rooted in their parents' own shame. Adults reared in dysfunctional families often complain of critical and demanding parents. They seldom received messages of unconditional acceptance. Their parents' self-hatred got passed to the child through endless demands and criticisms.[2]

The Perfect Fantasy

Lack of self-esteem may grow out of another trait: perfectionism. Children from dysfunctional homes develop a strong attraction to fantasy as a way of coping.[3] If Dad called his daughter a "slut" when he was drunk or assaulting her, she imagined herself to be a princess.

Adult children imagine what life would be like if their family didn't have its problem. They want to save the world . . . make it to Hollywood. Yet their impossible standards prevent true satisfaction. Until adult children discover the difference between excellence and perfectionism, they will continue to think badly about themselves most of the time.

Memories to Be Ashamed Of

The most simple explanation of the source of the adult child's shame is the intensity of disgraceful things that happened to her or him. Admitting that he lied from time to time, one member of our group explained, "It stems from being defensive. I am always sticking up for my parents and what they do or have done. Much comes from being embarrassed when I was a child because my parents would argue in public." An adult child's past is littered with disgraceful moments: seeing someone carry your drunken father up the porch steps . . . realizing your friends hear your parents scream at one another . . . looking out at the flashing lights of the police car in the driveway. When the disgrace is more private, as with sexual abuse, it may be even more shameful because the child is forced to handle it alone.

Co-dependency's Shameful Face

Some experts maintain that co-dependency is what creates shame and low self-esteem.[4] In the previous chapter, I explained how co-dependents become externally oriented— preoccupied with another person or circumstances outside themselves that inhibits development of self. Certainly all of us need to depend on one another to some extent; but not to the point where the dependence is obsessive, dominating our lives. Spending endless hours wondering whether or not Dad or Mom will be drunk is not the best stuff of childhood thoughts. According to one writer, "Co-dependents feel they have no intrinsic meaning of their own; almost all of their meaning comes from outside."

Being a co-dependent is like being stuck in your teen years, which is a time of self-discovery. The process of moving from childhood to adulthood establishes a personal identity that becomes a compass—a fixed point to which you refer when making countless decisions about getting through the forest of life.

This compass doesn't exist much during preadolescent childhood when you don't really have much of a sense of self apart from others, primarily because you don't have the mental capacity to stand back and look at yourself. That ability comes to most kids around the age of twelve or thirteen. Until then, a child lacks the ability to step outside of life and think about who he is.

When this new knack for thinking takes over, the emerging teen is struck with a severe case of self-consciousness. Life's most pressing issue is, "Who is this kid floating down the stream of life?" The teen looks inside at gifts, talents, and physical features, and uses things outside to provide a mirror to understanding self. Seeing a movie about starving Africans, a suburban sixteen-year-old girl begins to form an image of herself as a fairly wealthy middle-class American. Gradually, the teen chooses her surroundings to enhance the growing image of herself. If she begins to think of herself as an outgoing, people-related person instead of an intellectual bookworm, she becomes a cheerleader instead of a volunteer in the library.

Even her friends have to fit the picture slowly developing inside her skull. Thus, the cheerleader accepts dates only with jocks. To go out with a short, skinny computer whiz just wouldn't fit the image. While the teen is "finding herself," she will sometimes act like a chameleon. Not secure enough in her own identity, she will change colors to match those around her. Like trying on several pairs of jeans, she tries on one self after another in a frantic search for something that feels just right.

Note how much the teen is like the co-dependent. Externals are vital to the fragile, developing inner image. However, the teen will grow beyond heavy reliance on others. He or she will soon begin to see a personal self that is somewhat distinct from others, although others play a part. The teen must, for example, realize that she is a person apart from her parents. Parents will affirm her for her strengths and offer their opinions about her gifts and talents. But the parents' opinions and their presence won't always be necessary; they may even die. Therefore, to be healthy and mature she must learn to be herself apart from them and from others. As the picture develops, she can relate to others in a more mature way.

Take the matter of sex, for example. A young woman who has a secure sense of who she is sexually identifies being a woman with many things, not just having sex with a man. If she is insecure about what being a woman is, she may jump into bed with countless men in order to feel good about herself. She uses men, yet she is dependent on them. And because this is an illegitimate identity, she feels guilty and ashamed of who she is.

Sometimes dependence might be linked to the parent who is not drinking or abusing. Says one ACoA,

I don't think I was dependent upon my dad's feelings as much as my mother's. I don't remember asking my dad to stop drinking. But I frequently urged my mother to stop

yelling at him when he came home drunk. But it wasn't Dad that I would comfort. I would stumble into the attic where my mother went after fighting with Dad and try to comfort her. I would often do the dishes or scrub the floor to try to make her happy. This, of course, was a way of feeling good about myself; she really appreciated what I had done.

This is the fate of the co-dependent. What little self they have is easily given over to others—or to drugs or to vocations—because they feel like nothing without them. They are caught in a bind; they practice their addiction to feel good about themselves but in the process they feel worse. Not only do they have a low view of self, they have little view of self. It's like having a low supply of food in your cupboard while living by the handouts of others. Whenever the supply from the outside isn't there, you eat from your own little supply, but it doesn't satisfy. Thus, you try to find more outside help because of your own depleted resources.

Besides lacking outside sources, you may face a threat to your own food supply. Whenever anyone robs you, you feel devastated because you have so little left. This explains how adult children may be unable to handle neglect, disapproval, and loss of power and control.

The Shameful Lesson

Shame is also developed through the way we receive unspoken messages about ourselves. In many dysfunctional homes, the child's needs for self-esteem are not met because so much energy is spent on the dysfunctional person's needs. If his mother can't help him with his homework because she has gone to the local bar to look for Dad once again, the child receives the message, "You are not important."

For daughters, affirmation from the father is crucial to their sense of self as women. I once tried to help an overweight woman understand the basis of her lack of self-esteem. She admitted she didn't like herself and didn't see how she could be at all attractive. "When did you feel pretty?" I asked her.

"Once, when I got a special dress for a father-daughter banquet at our church."

"What happened?"

"This was just a few weeks after my dad left our home and filed for divorce. After getting the dress, I called to invite him to go with me, but he said he was too busy."

Out of all the memories she had of her dad this was the most vivid. In addition to rejection, she felt sure that he had left her mother because of the kids. In other words, her father had abandoned her and she never again felt attractive.

Anger, depression, fear, anxiety and other emotions or behaviors may be passed on in this way. Take for example, the fearful parent. He may overprotect the child, excessively warning of dangers out on the street or of possible future doom. Fear in the parent produces actions that yield fear in the child.

This explains why so many of us are like our parents even in areas we don't want to be—we could actually be trying to deal with the shame our parents possessed. This shame caused the parent to surround us with rigid rules, extreme punishment, and cruel judgments, along with a cold, nonloving relationship that instilled in us a compulsion to be perfect.

Poor Parents—Poor Me

Though I loved my dad, I grew up never wanting to be like him because of his drinking. It took quite a bit of effort for me to respect and honor him. Certainly, he had some fine traits that I could have and should have esteemed. But his alcoholism diminished them in my eyes.

Adult children from any kind of troubled home may have this same problem with a parent who may have been a successful judge, minister, mechanic, or pillar of the community. But his children knew of distorted sexual practices, foolish drunken gibberish, angry outbursts. The contrast between public and private life only intensified the shame.

Since children look to their parents as role models, and become somewhat like them, we can understand why it's difficult for persons from dysfunctional family to feel good about themselves. As one adult child says, "Every day I look in the mirror I see my father in me. Yet, I don't really respect my father. There is in me a part of myself I don't respect. I have even found myself resenting the way I laugh because I sound like him." This is one of the reasons we must learn to appreciate the good in our parents; in so doing, we will better appreciate ourselves.

The Shameful Secret

The most unique explanation for the adult child's shame is simply this: He or she grew up with a shameful "family secret." Family members knew something was wrong, yet no one talked about it. Any number of conditions qualify for being unmentionable: family violence, sexual assaults, problem drinking, possibly a lost job or relationship, or a period in a concentration camp or prison. Whitfield claims that keeping the family secret disables all members of the family, whether or not they know the secret.[5]

Every member of the alcoholic family masks reality with the illusion of normalcy. Each person works hard to keep up the image that everything is all right. The family can't control the angry or alcoholic parent, so it does the next best thing; it controls itself, maintaining the balance of the system by trying to ignore what is going on. When we don't face something because it is too humiliating, we bear that humiliation within. We don't feel the pain because we deny that it is so painful. As a result, we often don't help one another bear the burden we all carry.

One adult child of an alcoholic told her grown sister how she used to run up the stairs to her room when her drunken father went on a tirade. She slammed her door in an effort to slam out the frenzy below. Lonely and helpless, she wished her sister would have knocked on the door so they could comfort one another. Shocked by hearing this, her sister explained that she would follow her up the stairs, but because the door was closed, she would lie outside in the hallway feeling lonely and helpless, wishing her sister would open the door and let her in. That story, as the next, is sadly typical.

On warm summer days, my mother and dad shouted at each other; I would slip out of the house and go across the street near the neighbors' to see if the sound carried that far. It did. Though I was sure everyone knew about my dad's drinking, our family pretended it didn't exist. We never discussed it. I could never recall being comforted by an older brother or sister. I think I got a lot of my shame from my mother because I sensed she was so afraid we would be caught in public with my father while he was drunk. She seemed so concerned about what other people would think about us.

Even when my dad was about to check into a hospital treatment center, my mother tried to talk him out of it because she didn't want others to learn he was an alcoholic.

The silence and the denial only increase the sense of shame. It's like a patient not telling the doctor of his severe abdominal pain. By not admitting the problem, he denies himself the treatment.

Children with handicaps and problems that threaten their self-esteem, like having a huge purple birthmark or a speech impediment, learn that other people support and accept them despite what they think is a defect. Children from dysfunctional homes often do not get that same kind of support because they don't confront their problem in the right way. Denying what is happening in dysfunctional homes is the worst way of dealing with it. It creates a huge communication gap because the family doesn't talk about the one thing that matters the most to all of them.

GIVEN TO GUILT

Guilt is different from shame, but is closely related to it. Guilt, according to some people, is feeling bad about something you've done; shame is feeling bad about what you are. Counselors use this distinction to point out the serious, deeply felt nature of shame. Shame occupies the total self.

I can feel bad (guilty) about going fifty miles per hour past a thirty-five-mile-per-hour speed limit sign, particularly when a policeman stops to point it out to me. But I can own up to the crime and pay the fine and still feel okay about myself. It's not so easy to shake off shame about one's very being.

Distinguishing guilt from shame in this way makes sense, but it seems to ignore the more generally accepted definitions of the words. Shame is not just related to who we are; we can also feel ashamed about something we've done, just as we can feel guilty about it. The more usual distinction is this: guilt relates to laws; shame relates to people. Guilt grips us when we do something wrong— like stealing or lying. Shame occurs from doing something or being someone others would not respect. A person can feel both guilt and shame at being caught breaking a law, especially if he goes through the stop sign on his street and runs into his neighbor's car.

Adult children of alcoholics might have far more shame and guilt than other adults. Sandra Wilson's testing of adult children of alcoholics yielded convincing results. She found that evangelical Christian adult children of alcoholics are more guilt-prone and self-blaming, and more inclined to feel directly or indirectly responsible for the behavior of others than evangelical Christian adult children of nonalcoholics.[6]

Guilt is a powerful human emotion. It turns people into bundles of nerves and sends them to the hospital with physical complaints. It may make us criticize others to make ourselves feel better. Feeling God and others are angry with us, guilt may put us in a depressed state by telling us we are responsible even when we are not. An adult child told me she feels guilty when her children are bored, as if she must do something about it. Guilt might awaken us in the middle of the night, afraid of what the morning will bring. Some experts maintain it is the number one cause of psychological and emotional disorders.

Christians are blessed with the remedy for guilt. Because Christ died for us, we are free from condemnation. Yet some Christians still feel guilty. This kind of guilt may have a cause, but it is not a legitimate one.

You're Ok, I'm Not

One of the most vivid ways of explaining how we got our guilt is offered by Barbara Wood, co-founder of a clinic that specializes in the treatment of co-dependency. She claims that adult children deal with the negative side of their parents by taking it inside themselves. She points to the thinking of W. R. D. Fairbairn: He had spent part of his career as a counselor working with delinquent children who, he said, came "from homes which the most casual observer could hardly fail to recognize as *bad* in the crudest sense—homes, for example, in which drunkenness, quarreling, and physical violence reigned supreme." Wood explains: "He was struck by the refusal of these children to characterize their parents as *bad* and by the intensity of their devotion to mothers and fathers who were both neglectful and abusive. He found that children who would not accuse the worst parents of bad behavior would easily accuse themselves of being bad children." Fairbairn concluded that mistreated children coped with terrible circumstances by taking into themselves the badness of their parents. "The child would rather be bad himself than have bad objects . . . and one of his motives in becoming bad is to make his objects *good*."[7]

Children want to rid themselves of the flaws they see in their parents because they need to maintain a relationship with them. Parents are their major source of love and usually their only source of protection. They have no option but to get all the warmth they can from them. They need to make the best of a bad situation. Fairbairn claims that as far as the child is able to purge his parents of their badness, he is rewarded by the sense of security that a good environment confers. It's a way of maintaining some control, of surviving. The battle scars are often false guilt and low self-esteem.

Wood describes Rita as an example. "Rita discovered early on that the tenderness she craved and the brutality she feared came in the same bewildering and terrifying package. One of her mother's frequent alcoholic rituals involved beating Rita with a piece of clothesline until the child's back was covered with bleeding welts and then confining her to her room. Sometime later, the mother would knock at the door of her daughter's room and issue an affectionate invitation to join her in baking a batch of cookies. Rita always accepted this invitation, and when she did, her mother would take her gently by the hand and lead her to the kitchen. It is critical to note that Rita did not lie in bed dreading her mother's return after these beatings, but, rather, lay there praying for the knock on the door that signaled the possibility of approach."[8]

The Child's Blame Game

Dysfunctional parents contribute to the problem by heaping blame upon their children. "You're the cause of all the problems around here," is a rough statement for an eleven-year-old girl to deal with. Directly or indirectly, they feel responsible. "My dad left my mom because of me," or "If I behaved differently, Mom wouldn't drink." The sexually abused may think, "I feel guilty because there are times I responded sexually to my dad's assaults." "I can't get over the guilt I feel for sometimes feeling close to my mother when she fondled me." We adults know children shouldn't feel guilty when things happen they can't control. But it's not so obvious to children.

Mixed messages create guilt and a sense of worthlessness. When the alcoholic father doesn't show up for the baseball game like he promised, he sends a mixed signal: "I say I care, but I don't." A few days ago a girl told me about her brother. Home for the summer after one year at a prominent college, his alcoholic father promptly told him he would not be able to return. Pretending to be too poor, he insisted he attend a local junior college while living at home. At the end of the summer, the father said to him in front of the family at the supper table, "You may go back to your college." He then lied, "We can't afford it; we will all have to eat less food and cut down in other ways." Resisting, her brother said he was willing to study at the local school. But the father insisted that he pack up and leave. Confused and heavy-hearted, he did.

Even if parents didn't force you to blame yourself, you may have done so because of your childish thinking. Young children have a notion about magic. They feel very powerful. Like the magicians and superpersons they read about, they think they, too, can perform amazing feats like stopping Mom from drinking or Dad from getting angry. When they fail, they may feel guilty.

Another reason for childish guilt is the under-developed sense of cause and effect. They may not see clearly why things happen. Abuse and alcoholism are mysterious behaviors anyway. After drinking on Monday, a father may promise with great remorse not to do it again, but is drunk again on Wednesday. The child can easily begin to think that something he is doing or not doing is causing his father to drink. Seeing how bad drinking is, the child feels that he has done something wrong.

Guilt is a major problem when there is sexual abuse. A girl may blame herself for her father's attacks. She may think she seduced him by wearing short skirts or being too attractive. If her body responds or she feels close to him during sex, she feels more like a participant in something wrong than a victim of something detestable. Though it's clear to other people that abuse has taken place, it is not always clear to the abused. A counselor recently reminded her sexually abused client that she was a victim. The client replied, "Would you tell me that often? I have such a hard time believing that."

The Parent's Blame Game

Parents who victimize may blame the victim in an effort to excuse themselves. The sexual abuser blames the child for doing something to turn him on, or the parent blames the child for her drinking. Said one woman, "When I was as young as twelve, my drunken father would sometimes keep me up all night long, ranting and raving about how I was to blame for the problems in the family." Assaults like these are bound to cause guilt and shame that might still be felt decades afterwards.

A FEARFUL FOCUS

Along with guilt, adult children seem to be unusually afraid. In his personal journal, one adult child wrote:

Right now I am really shaky. I am afraid of something. I can't get a hold of what I am afraid of—most perplexing. Is the cause of my fear my dad's maniacal behavior? What, may I ask, am I afraid of? My God, why can't I be normal? I hurt.

The adult child's fear may be more frequent than other adults', and the objects of his fear are different. Perhaps the major fear is that of losing control.[9] As parents, adult children may be terribly afraid of losing control of their children, and this may make them unusually strict. In any of their relationships, control can be an issue—how much a person controls a discussion or a spouse controls the marriage. Fear was created by having to cope with a chaotic, unpredictable life in a dysfunctional family. Loss of control there meant harsh beatings, long evenings listening to screaming parents. Or it meant grave disappointment. They learned not to trust.

The control issue may also show up in difficulty with relating to people in authority, either fearing them or resisting them. To their insecurity add their distrust of others, particularly parental figures, and you can see why they may feel frightened and angry when a boss tells them what to do or a policeman pulls them over for speeding. Since God is the ultimate parental figure, some adult children have trouble relating to Him.

They may also fear being like their parents. If the adult child of an alcoholic drinks alcohol, he or she may do so with grave fear of becoming addicted and losing control. Likewise the adult abused in childhood harbors a great fear of losing his temper and hurting his child.

ABNORMAL ANXIETY

Fear takes its most insidious form in a feeling of dread, of anxiety. It arouses us on our beds and whispers to us that something terrible is about to happen. Anxiety is a typical problem for all adults. It has been called the official emotion of our age. It gnaws at us, squelching energy and destroying good feelings. It distracts us, causing our concentration to flit from place to place like a parakeet let loose in a house. Sometimes it comes over us in uncontrollable ways, and may last for days, weeks, or even years.

Fear and anxiety are much alike. The body reacts the same to both: rapid and unusually strong heartbeat, rapid or shallow breathing, trembling, sweating, muscular tension, dryness of the mouth, changes in voice quality, and faintness. Each can heighten blood pressure, create an upset stomach and intense headaches. Yet anxiety differs from fear. We fear whenever we face (or think we face) a real danger. Whenever we are afraid and don't know why, we are anxious.

All of us suffer from some anxiety simply because we are human and, to some degree, helpless. People from troubled homes suffer more than usual. The cause of the fear and anxiety may be forgotten or buried deeply in the mind. Sometimes adult children experience trauma from triggered flashbacks to these forgotten incidents, like veterans of war.

The Danger Zone Called Home

Tracing anxiety to a dysfunctional home is rather simple. If today you have a feeling that doom is just around the corner, it may be because you lived through a time when it actually was. You were never sure when some new disaster might take place. And often you were protected from it by the rest of the family. One man explained:

One night my father came home with a swollen, blackening injury to his face and eye. Several teeth were broken and his mouth was bloody. Being only seven or eight years old, I was frightened and sorry. But, no one would tell me what had happened to him. It wasn't until a day or so later that my mother told me someone had punched him. I had to do more asking of others to find out it happened in a bar down the street. I can remember being frightened and ashamed whenever I walked past the place.

Kept in the Dark

Sharon Wegscheider-Cruse claims that extreme anxiety may be bred in the child of the alcoholic family called the "mascot."[10] The "baby" of the family, this child is protected by the other family members. "Parents and older siblings take great care to screen what they say to this child. They do not tell him about Susie's abortion or Tony's smoking dope or the fact that Mom and Dad do not sleep together any more. When he asks questions about what is going on in the family, he is answered, not with information, but with vague reassurances."[11] All this overprotecting damages the child, who obviously feels something is going on. Suspicions create fear which turn into anxiety when the child is not given the facts to explain this fear. When he grows up, anxiety becomes his characteristic emotion. Yet the mascot masks it by playing the part of the clown to please his family and friends. Because he doesn't cope properly with the internal pain, his life and problems may become unbearable. And because of his superficiality, he will fail to develop his full potential, pretending life is just a lark.

Anxious Parent/Anxious Child

It's possible we got our anxiety less from the events of our home and more from the persons around us. We watched and imitated them, often unconsciously. As I mentioned in the last chapter, we usually copy the same sex parent, but not always. Usually it's the parent we have the closest relationship with. If a boy identifies with an alcoholic father, he may feel and act out his dad's emotions and behaviors. This could account for why sons— more often than daughters—of alcoholic fathers become alcoholics. Since anxiety is basic to any addict's existence, the child picks that up with a lot of other emotions and behaviors related to the addict's lifestyle.

Anxiety may be "caught" from the nonalcoholic or nonabusing parent. This was the case with one man:

My wife and I decided that I identified more with my mother than my alcoholic father. She often said to me, "You worry just like your mother did." Both of us wished I had been more like my dad in this respect. He joked more, laughed more.

Anxiety can be picked up more from the co-dependent than the addict, since the addict may worry less. The addict drowns his or her anxiety in drink, drugs, work, or food, making his or her roller coaster lifestyle somewhat tolerable. The co-dependent endures the ups and downs soberly, strapped on board with no control, worrying about how far down the next slope will go. The co-dependent suffers the most. A divorced woman forced to depend on the support payments of her alcoholic husband is the one to lose the most when he loses his job. Though she gives no support for it, Anne Schaef claims, "We now know that co-dependence results in such physical complications as gastrointestinal problem ulcers, high blood pressure, and even cancer. Indeed, the co-dependent will often die sooner than the chemically dependent person."[12] No wonder. The abuser vents his hostile feelings when things go wrong. The sexual offender gets some pleasure, however perverted. The addict has the beloved chemical to soothe his nerves. But the co-dependent is left with the mess, the pain, and the heartbreak, unless he or she learns to break free.

BEING DOWN

Though depression is probably the most common kind of abnormal emotion today, it occurs more in adult children than in other adults. Some therapists view depression as anger turned in upon oneself. Adult children might easily swallow their anger because their love for their parents keeps them from permitting themselves to admit it's really there.

One explanation not yet mentioned is especially connected with depression. A cadre of experts believe adult children are like they are because they are grieving the loss of their childhood. They feel deprived of the kind of family life they see others having. To overcome their past they need to proceed through the grieving process, which has clearly defined stages: denial (not admitting anything was wrong in the family), bargaining (trying to make it all balance out by what you promise yourself or God), getting angry (permitting yourself to be upset by your losses), depression (going through the sadness that comes when you realize your can't recover your loss), acceptance (acknowledging the loss as something you can live with). Unfortunately many adult children get stuck in one stage or another. Treatment consists of identifying the stage you are in and helping your grief take its course.

WHY RESOLVES ONE AND TWO ARE DIFFICULT

Admitting to ourselves that we have problems is difficult to do. Shying away from the truth about ourselves protects us from the shock of being exposed too suddenly to our darker, weaker side. Yet we can protect ourselves too much and too long. Many in Jesus' day refused His remedies because they denied their need for them. To them He said, "It is not the healthy who need a doctor, but the sick."

Feeling that we are unable to do anything about a problem, we simply ignore it. This, too, has its roots in our past. Bucking up against insurmountable family problems, we learned to feel helpless. Unable to face and to solve the problem, we coped with it by escaping from it.

The members of our support group see this tactic regularly. We receive telephone calls from adult children who tell us of terrible childhoods but they never show up at our meetings. Sometimes they meet with us for several sessions, tell their stories and give us a glimpse of their depression and personal struggles, and then drop out. When asked why, their answers usually betray their denial: "My problems aren't that bad"; "I can't take the time to face them now."

Being honest with ourselves is the first step of recovery. In Christ, we reject deception as a way of feeling good about ourselves. We replace it with hope, because in Him we know that things can be different. "You shall know the truth, and the truth shall make you free" (John 8:32, NASB). Though Jesus was speaking of the gospel, what he said applies to all truth. Any truth can be liberating. Because the Christian's greatest asset is truth, he above all persons should not be afraid of it. If the truth turns out to be sin, he can confess it. If it turns out to be evil, he can have victory over it. The worst thing we can do with truth is deny it.

BENEFITS OF RESOLVES ONE AND TWO

Adult children are usually ecstatic when they open their eyes to the negative impact of their troubled childhood family. It is such a relief to finally understand what they have been fighting against. This was true of the Christian young man I visited in a hospital psychiatric ward. He was there for an attempted suicide. Prior to the night he swallowed the pills, he had tried to cope with self-contempt and depression due in part to a notoriously bad family background. Yet most people advised him to forget about the past.

Apparently many people believe that if you blame your problems on the past you are only excusing yourself and wallowing in self-pity. But forgetting about his past was the worst thing this man could do; it stripped him of any inner strength and left him with intense feelings of failure and self-hate that drove him to try to end his life.

When you connect your present struggles to your past, you deal a terrific blow to guilt and self-loathing. You may have been working on some of your weaknesses for years, with limited success. You've felt bad about your struggles and your failure. But now that you have seen the powerful influence of your childhood, you may be less inclined to be so hard on yourself. This happened to Mike after a few sessions in our group.

Once I started to talk, the feelings of relief started to flow. The people I was with listened intently, and I felt that at least I could now understand better why I am the way I am. To have come from an alcoholic home was not my fault. Somewhere deep down inside I had been feeling guilty about my family. Now I knew that it was okay to be different.

Shifting the cause to your parents is not the same as shifting the blame. We are not trying to accuse but to explain. When we do, we tend to feel less guilty about our faults and more patient about our efforts to rid ourselves of them.

This new perspective will do a lot of things for you. You will obviously understand better why you do what you do, particularly if you can see clearly that you are acting out some role you adopted in childhood. Maybe you now understand why you knock yourself out to please other people, or why you pour yourself out for others.

Seeing yourself more accurately should help you see others more accurately. If, for example, you admit to being hypercritical, your friends, spouse, or children will start to look a lot better to you. You'll also be more inclined to see your good qualities, because you can look at your achievements and traits in the light of the handicaps of your background. Though you'll see the bad side of your survival tactics, you'll see the good side as well.

Being a pleaser, for example, you may have taken too much responsibility for others and neglected your own interests and comforts to a fault; but it may also have made you a kind, considerate person whom God has used. One woman, an ACoA, was deeply disappointed when she learned that adult children of alcoholics often become servants to others. She had thought her desire to help people was due to the gift of "helps" given by the Holy Spirit. Now she had begun to look down on this unselfishness. Instead, she should recognize that an all-powerful God can use our backgrounds to conform us to Himself and enhance any trait with the supernatural gift from the Holy Spirit. She can thank God for the positive side of her co-dependency pattern while trying to escape from the harmful effects.

There are times when awareness of a problem actually solves it. One excited adult child tells what happened when he made the connection between a feeling of dread and his childhood life in an alcoholic family: "It lost its power. Sure, I still have my fears, but they don't resemble the monster I battled for decades. Whenever he comes along, I just tell him I'm done with him because I have put away childish things."

REACTIONS TO RESOLVES ONE AND TWO

The awareness stage is not always pleasant. Like surgery, its benefits come with pain. Facing your past will put you in touch with repressed feelings. Though the idea that we repress our feelings is a theory, it seems to fit our emotional experience. Suppose it is possible to actually block from consciousness feelings too painful to admit. A person might even go so far as to forget the events that caused these feelings.

As a child, for example, you may have felt such shame when your father screamed obscenities at you that you denied you felt that way. Or else, you felt such hurtful guilt because you thought you did something to make your mother get drunk that you dismissed it from your memory. As a child, you just can't handle it properly. You tuck it away into the back of your mind. However, when you stuff it down into the unconscious part of you, it still has power over you—in the form of depression or guilt.

With the help of her counselor one woman discovered that her bad feelings toward herself came from repressed feelings of shame when she watched her father beat her brothers severely with his belt. When this shame popped to the surface of her mind, she could now handle it in an adult way.[13]

If it's possible to bury feelings inside, it's easy to see how terribly painful and even risky it can be to dredge them up, since they had to be grossly intense to be buried in the first place.

While you've read the first chapters of this book your mind has made quite a few trips back to your childhood. You've no doubt dug up some buried feelings and forgotten memories. One member of our group expressed the pain and confusion he was feeling during the first months of our meetings. Talking about the past was like putting a spoon into the bottom of his soul and stirring up what had settled there. "I have been so overwhelmed by feelings during the past few weeks," he told us. "I have been tempted to stop attending the meetings, but I have to get on with this." This is typical of adult children in the first years of recovery. You may begin to feel like a volcano about to erupt. As you recall repressed memories of childhood, you may have what experts call "Spontaneous Age Regression." As you recall your childhood, you relive it; you become a child again.[14] People report feeling hurt, angry, depressed and often quite confused. The survivors of some homes are like survivors of war or concentration camps. Recall of the past can produce severe stress and shock. The dangers of such flashbacks are one reason why many adult children need the presence of a group or a counselor during recovery.

Reactions are not always so severe, but they can be very powerful. It's not uncommon for adult children in recovery to feel like they are six years old again. While I was first reliving my childhood a few years ago, I had a strange, intense experience. It happened one summer while my wife and I were camping together. She had gone to gather some wood and I was left alone. Suddenly, a vivid memory of my mother and father hit me. I was so overwhelmed that I began to weep and then spontaneously pretended to talk with them. I brought up matters we had never discussed. I told them how I loved and appreciated them, trying to recapture the past and say things I wish had passed my childish lips.

Part of my reaction was no doubt caused by grief. Sorrow may be a repeated feeling during your days of recovery if your parents are not living. You will grieve over your losses as you become aware that you may not have had a father's word of praise . . . a mother's comforting hug . . . a peaceful home . . . family fun times.

One group member talked of his lost adolescence. He had spent his youth on drugs and alcohol, associating with other burned-out teens. He couldn't recall having a happy, proper date with a teenage girl. He never asked one out because his poor self-image made him scared she would say no. When he realized this, he had an intense desire to date young girls. Though he was nearly thirty and had no intention of striking up any serious relationship, he decided to try dating some of the girls at a nearby college. All he wanted was an evening of wholesome fun and companionship. He wanted to relive his youth and reclaim some of the losses.

I heard of a whole support group that tried to reclaim one of their childhood losses. After learning that none of them ever had children stay overnight at their homes, they staged a big pajama party, staying up most of the night playing games and talking.

Recovery may also arouse some anger with God. You may feel cheated because God didn't seem to protect you when you were a child. Or you may think He failed you because you had problems for so long. The voice inside says, "Now that I have some solutions to my problems, why did it take me so long to find them?" Adult children sometimes complain, "Why didn't these problems go away when I placed my faith in Christ?" We need to learn to praise Him for enabling us to cope with these matters in a way we might not have been able to do without Him. And we thank Him for the new insights that are helping us.

Becoming More Aware

There are some practical ways to get a more accurate picture of your childhood. Try writing a personal biography over a period of time. When you search your mind for details about your grade school classes, teachers, playmates, etc., try reflecting on what was going on in your home and how you were feeling. Talk with others who knew you and your family. Relatives and neighbors can help you get a more accurate picture. Take some imaginary trips back to your past. Try imagining what it was like being six years old, and try to get in touch with what your feelings were then.

Admitting the power of the past and getting the skeletons out of the closet is only the first step. We might be overwhelmed by the emotions we feel and the changes we must make, but what hope we have for recovery is based primarily on our next resolve.

Notes

1. Craig Ellison, "Self-Esteem: An Overview," *Your Better Self*, ed. Craig W. Ellison (New York: Harper & Row, Publishers, 1983), p. 4.

2. Fossum and Mason, p. 112.

3. Marlin, p. 12.

4. Anne Wilson Schaef, *Co-Dependence: Misunderstood—Mistreated* (San Francisco: Harper & Row, Publishers, 1986), p. 44.

5. Whitfield, pp. 47-48.

6. Wilson, p. 59

7. W. R. D. Fairbairn, "The Repression and the Return of Bad Objects," in *Psychoanalytic Studies of the Personality*, ed. W. R. D. Fairbairn, p. 65, cited by Barbara L. Wood, *Children of Alcoholism: The Struggle for Self and Intimacy in Adult Life* (New York: University Press, 1987), p. 23.

8. Wood, p. 54.

9. Marlin, pp. 20-21.

10. Wegscheider-Cruse, *Another Chance*, pp. 137-49.

11. Ibid., p. 138.

12. Schaef, p. 6.

13. Fossum and Mason, p. 155.

14. Patricia O'Gorman and Philip Oliver-Diaz, *Breaking the Cycle of Addiction: A Parent's Guide to Raising Healthy Kids* (Pompano Beach, FLA.: Health Communications, Inc., 1987), p. 13.

RESOLVE

We resolve to trust God,
not ourselves, as we,
with the support of others,
attempt to change.

5

Practicing Dynamics of Recovery

Those who work closely with adult children, even those from so-called secular agencies, almost always mention a spiritual dimension to recovery. In ACoA and other groups associated with Alcoholics Anonymous, the first three steps affirm this reliance on God.

Step one: "We admitted we were powerless over alcohol—that our lives had become unmanageable."

Step two: "(We) came to believe that a power greater than ourselves could restore us to sanity."

Step three: "(We) made a decision to turn our will and our lives over to the care of God as we understood Him."

Christian critics of these groups blame them for not being more specific about who God is, leaving that choice to the individual.

While we Christians would decidedly define God as the God and Father of our Lord Jesus Christ, we can still see something positive in the spiritual emphasis of these groups. First, they permit Christians the freedom to believe and to express their own beliefs; and second, they provide further proof of man's need for God as affirmed in Scripture. The physicians, psychologists, and social workers who insist that addicted persons and their families need a "higher power" are making a remarkable admission that we can't succeed without God.

Francis of Assisi mentioned two types of problems when he prayed, "Lord, give us the serenity to accept the things we cannot change and the courage to change the things we can, and the wisdom to know the difference." A parent's rejection, mistreatment, neglect, or drinking are things that may never change; our only recourse is to accept them through God's power.

Trust is a moment by moment experience based on God's promise of power to those who trust Christ as Savior. The apostle Paul prayed that Christians might know God's incomparable "great power for us who believe." He then described the power as "like the working of his mighty strength, which he exerted in Christ when he raised him from the dead and seated him at his right hand in the heavenly realms" (Ephesians 1:19-20).

God's power is turned on to us only when we rely on Him. This is why, day by day, we must face each moment trusting Him and not our own resources. There's a wonderful freedom for those who let go and let God.

Trust Is Both Solution and Problem

Some of your adult child traits will work against you in   your spiritual life. A study of ACoAs supported our suspicion that evangelical adult children of alcoholics have more problems than other evangelicals with trusting God's will and believing biblical promises regarding God's care.[1] This gives the recovery process an ironic twist: Trusting God is part of the solution as well as part of the problem.

There is no easy answer to this. It is possible that once you link your general inability to trust to your past, you will begin to have some relief from your doubting of God. Your alcoholic father may have deceived your family, but you can say to yourself, "God is not a man, that He should lie" (Numbers 23:19). You may not have been able to trust your parents' promises, but, "Let us hold unswervingly to the hope we profess, for he who promised is faithful" (Hebrews 10:23). You may have blamed yourself when your father disappointed you, but you can recall, "If we are faithless, he will remain faithful" (2 Timothy 2:13).

Our trust in God must be radical. We must refuse to trust ourselves. The joke about the man who slipped off the edge of a cliff makes the point deftly.

> Hanging by a branch of a small shrub he clutched on the way down, the man looked up and yelled, "Is there anyone up there?" There was no answer. He yelled again, "Is anyone up there?" Silence again. A third cry got a response.
>
> "Yes," said the booming voice.
>
> "Who is it?" shouted the cliff hanger.
>
> "It's me, God."
>
> "Help me," the desperate man shouted, his arm tiring.
>
> "Okay," said the voice, "let go of the branch."
>
> A long silence followed. Then, in a voice more desperate than ever came the plea, "Is there anyone else up there?"

As adult children, we have a terrible time letting go and letting God. Yet, in that day by day, hour by hour surrender lies our peace and hope. Through His power, not ours, we will eventually find the freedom from our past we so desperately seek.

TRUSTING IS NO SUBSTITUTE FOR TRYING

Your attitude of mistrust and your hurt feelings don't vanish easily, so be prepared for a struggle. True, when there is nothing we can do about a situation, we can only rest in God's will. But whenever we can do something, we can set out to do it—not in our strength, but in His. To trust isn't something we do by sitting on our hands, waiting for God to act; it is something we do while we act.

When young David faced the giant, he provided us a lasting example of true faith. When he refused to wear King Saul's armor and sword to battle Goliath, he was not showing us that trust in God is enough—as if God would take care of Goliath without David's own efforts. David refused Saul's armor because he had never used it before. Clumsily stumbling out to face a huge veteran warrior with the same uniform and weapons the giant was expert in using would have taken a whole lot more faith than what he chose to do. He took his sling, which he was skilled in using, because it provided the best chance of winning. It was not a lesser weapon than a sword, but a better one. Yet he didn't place his trust in his slingshot. To Goliath he said, "I come against you in the name of the LORD Almighty, the God of the armies of Israel, whom you have defied. This day the LORD will hand you over to me" (1 Samuel 17:45-46).

Perhaps you have heard it said that we should pray as if it all depended upon God and work as if it all depended upon us. Actually, whether we work or pray, we trust in God alone. When we move out, God moves in us. Paul put it well: "I worked harder than all of them—yet not I, but the grace of God that was with me" (1 Corinthians 15:10).

GOD WORKS IN US THROUGH OTHERS

Besides looking to God for power to change, we also look to others, not as a substitute for God but as a channel of His power. We confess we cannot recover alone. God's people provide all sorts of dynamics for our growth: rebuke, correction, comfort, encouragement, acceptance, truth, love. (2 Timothy 2:2; 2 Corinthians 1:4; Romans 15:7; Ephesians 4:15, 16). Others can help us escape the consequences of our sins: "Confess your sins to each other and pray for each other so that you may be healed" (James 5:16). Christians play a part in restoring us whenever we are "caught in a sin" (Galatians 6:1-2). We fulfill the law of Christ whenever we "carry each other's burdens." Scripture makes it clear that whenever we interact with God's people we are in touch with God's power.

If you haven't yet told someone about the abuse you have suffered, do so. If you think your abuse was especially severe or if it was of a sexual nature, you should be careful to reveal this only to someone trained to handle these matters. Your counselor will probably send you to a support group.

Even without personal counseling, you may benefit from joining a group that specializes in your type of problem. I've listed some in the back of the book. Some groups, like Overeaters Anonymous and Sexaholics Anonymous, deal with specific behaviors. Some center on the childhood family: Adult Children of Alcoholics, (and adults from other types of dysfunctional families) and FACES (for formerly abused young adults). Usually, these groups will not force their religious viewpoint on you since they accept people of all faiths. Because of the spiritual and biblical issues involved, many churches and individual Christians are beginning groups with a biblical emphasis, although they encourage their members to also attend other groups as a Christian presence and to benefit from the group's expertise.

If there is no group in your area, it's simple to start one. Contact a pastor or counselor who can assist you. Or begin a group yourself. A call or letter to the national headquarters of one of these groups will put all the materials into your hands (see Appendix for information). It will take just one more person for you to get a group going. If at all possible, arrange for people to meet in a place where there is little chance of their being known. A church or community organization will no doubt gladly supply a room for you.

Be Careful Whom You Lean On

Resist the urge to rely on just anyone as a support person. After reading books like this, adult children often get so excited about sorting out the past and tackling their problems that they share their ideas and dump their feelings on anyone close by, usually a close friend, spouse, or child. Though these loved ones care, they may not fully grasp what you are talking about and may not give the kind of feedback you hoped for. They may become weary of the subject and even fearful of your honest self-disclosures. While you will have some things to share with these loved ones, be cautious about leaning too heavily on them. You will need to show them you are changing instead of always talking about it.

What Groups Offer

Support groups provide special help for us. Because the members are suffering from the same kinds of experiences, they provide a safe place to expose very personal things. Many of the events and pains of the past lie secretly hidden inside us like rotting apples in the corner of a dark, cold cellar; the odor eventually fills the basement and filters into the upper rooms. Unlike apples, our secrets will not quietly decay into nothing, but they rapidly decompose when brought into the light and air. Shame and hurt thrive in darkness; they can't seem to stand the light of day. If you were sexually abused only once, and it is back there in a crevice of your memory, you may find release just by talking about it.

The love and acceptance in support groups is special. Ordinarily we receive acceptance from people who don't fully know about our struggles and backgrounds. In a group you discover that people hold you in regard no matter how scandalous and shameful your story may seem to you. Someone put it well: "There is no peace, no matter the facade they put on, for those who deep down inside themselves have a fear of being known." When you are loved, even though you are known, you will have a new-found peace.

One woman told about her first visit to an ACoA group. Wandering the halls of the church looking for the meeting, she finally found a room with people in it. After entering she was sure it was the wrong meeting. "People were so well dressed and attractive looking, I was sure they couldn't be adult children; I thought it was a meeting of the church council. Too embarrassed to tell them the kind of group I was looking for, I turned around to walk out. Just as I did a woman asked me if I was looking for the ACoA group. I was jolted when she told me this was it."

A group helps validate your experience. Lurking in every adult child's mind is the question of whether or not he or she is blowing things out of proportion. When you tell your story, others help you think more accurately about it. You may find others agreeing that you truly were a victim. They will also help you remember. During meetings you will recall things you long ago forgot; bringing them to your consciousness will help you deal with them.

One of my students, born out of wedlock by a mother who eventually married twice, both times to alcoholics, said, "I still get emotional when I think of my childhood, and I don't like to talk about it to others except when I want to speak cynically about alcoholics." We need to talk about how we feel, even if our only speech is sarcastic, harsh, and hateful. As we talk seriously about our feelings, we can better overcome them and see more objectively what happened to us and to our parents.

Break the Silence

You'll have to overcome inner resistance to joining a group or seeing a counselor. If you've kept your secret for a long time, there are reasons why you have done so. First of all, there is the shame. Our culture attaches a stigma to child abuse, alcoholism, incest, and child neglect. Even though they shouldn't, the victim often shares the disgrace of the offender. Christians should have less hesitation than others about joining a group, since confessing our sins to others is a normal concept to us (James 5:16). If we are to confess when we have done wrong, how much easier should it be to tell when we have *been* wronged.

The desire to protect your parents will haunt your efforts to expose your past. A sexually abused woman who wrote about her story under another name explains her mixed feelings: "I have a great fear of the story," she writes. "My relationship with my parents is very fine these days, and I fear that someday, sometime, they will come across it. I still want to protect them."[2] She feels this way even though her father did hideous sexual things to her many years ago. This desire to protect runs very deep in families. Certainly our parents have a right to some privacy, but seeing a counselor need not be attached to them in any way.

Support groups try to protect members and families in various ways, such as using first names only. But protection should not require denying ourselves badly needed help. That only perpetuates the childish sacrificing of self for a problem parents refuse to face.

Almost all of our group members attend our group without telling their parents. Eventually the question about whether or not to tell does come up. We recognize there isn't one answer for everyone. We conclude that it depends on whether or not your telling will be beneficial for either yourself or your parents.

Letting an alcoholic family know you are in a group for adult children may be one more way to help them face their problem if they are in denial. There are times when the family needs to know you have been hurt, and as we will see later, there are times when it helps you for them to know.

IN YOUR RESOLVE TO CHANGE, MAKE HASTE SLOWLY

The word *change* will get a mixed reception from adult children. On the one hand, many of them want so badly to be different; on the other, change often frustrates and overwhelms them. The intensity it takes to understand yourself and grow, coupled with group work, often creates the need to "back off" and relax for a while, especially in the beginning of recovery.

To make your journey through the rest of this book a bit less difficult and a bit more profitable, take the following ideas about change with you.

Change Is Christian

A Christian person is a changing person. God will have it no other way. Every chapter of the New

Testament shouts with the idea of change. "I press on toward the goal," blazoned the apostle Paul, even while in prison. "All of us who are mature should take such a view of things," he claimed. A sign of being mature is knowing you are not. Those who have come a long way know they have a long way to go. This is our hope. God doesn't just demand we change by loading us down with commands; he promises change by freeing us to abundant life. "Now the Lord is the Spirit, and where the Spirit of the Lord is, there is freedom. And we, who with unveiled faces all reflect the Lord's glory, are being transformed into his likeness with ever-increasing glory, which comes from the Lord, who is the Spirit" (2 Corinthians 3:17, 18). "Being transformed" is present tense; we are ever to "grow in the grace and knowledge of our Lord and Savior Jesus Christ" (2 Peter 3:18).

Change Is Human

Life is dynamic. Adult children especially need to be alert to this, since a problem we think we have handled today may trouble us later. Take being intimate, for example. You may have lived down a lot of your inhibitions, freeing yourself to share your feelings with friends in the dorm room or the office.

But marriage may slam the issue in your face again. After dealing with it for a while in marriage and feeling some success, having a child may bring it up again. There is no status quo. But that's not a threat; it's a challenge which God Himself accepts.

Change Is from God

The phrase "are being transformed" is a passive form. If it were active, it would say "We are transforming ourselves." Instead, it tells us God is changing us. Lean on Him and be patient while He does His work in you.

Change Is toward Maturity

As there are numerous explanations for the way adult children come by their problems, there are a number of systems for getting them out of them. One of these is adopted in the twelve step program for adult children. We recover "gradually by gently loving ourselves as we mature and by allowing our inner child to grow up."[3] The inner child is not merely the immature part of you. It is the genuine self, whose growth was stunted by your childhood family.

I see no reason why the Christian cannot accept this dazzling concept, at least in part. Growth, for us, comes from a healthy environment that permits us to be ourselves instead of a damaging one that forces us to conform at the expense of our true selves. "I am discovering a talent and joy in oil painting," a thirty-year-old adult child told me last week. Scoffing at all art forms, forbidding him any expression, his strict parents had kept the artist within to the size of a dwarf. Breaking free, his inner child began to grow. This book aims to foster that kind of growth.

In addition to looking inside themselves for guidance, Christians have another place to look. In 2 Corinthians 3:18, Paul credits transformation to reflecting the Lord's glory. The term *to reflect* also means "to contemplate," suggesting Paul had this double meaning in mind. As the Christian focuses his attention on the radiant Christ, he projects that radiance, all the while becoming more and more like Him. This was God's plan for us when He created us in His likeness. It is now salvation's goal that we "put on the new self, which is being renewed in knowledge in the image of its Creator" (Colossians 3:10). We are not left to ourselves to determine our true authenticity. Day by day we become more authentic as we aim toward Christlike qualities of love, joy, peace, patience, kindness, goodness, faithfulness, gentleness and self-control.

Change Is Risky

Basking in the promise of change, we sometimes overlook its risks. The actions suggested in the following chapters may look like impossible feats of daring. Just the thought of trusting others, giving up control, sharing your deepest feelings, asking for help, rewarding yourself and being more flexible may make you shiver. Yet, the hope of the gospel is that we should expect something different from ourselves, that none of us is so emotionally handicapped that we cannot become more Christlike.

Yet change requires that you plunge headlong into the realm of the uncomfortable. One man in our group so deeply felt that he would be rejected if he asked a woman for a date that he hadn't taken a girl out for twelve years, though he desperately wanted to. Encouraged by our group, he resolved to risk doing so. In the next meeting, he excitedly reported that he had invited a girl to go out with him. She turned him down. Still, he was elated because the rejection was not nearly as hard to take as he had imagined. The next time we met, he told us he had dared to ask another, this time with success.

Being afraid of failure and seeing things in black and white terms make risktaking hard for adult children. We may inject these attitudes into our Christian faith—because God is Lord of our lives, we will want only to do what is clearly right and guaranteed to succeed. It may be hard for us to see that some boundaries are not so clearly marked by God and that we sometimes have to tread uncertain paths, finding His will as we move along. Some of the most dramatic changes in my life came when I said to myself, "Here goes. I'll give it a try and see what happens." Unless we learn to do that we will always be stuck in the status quo, paralyzed by our fears.

Risktakers also have to tolerate the fallout that comes from their decisions and actions. When you venture into new territory, you may release a flood of guilt, fear, anxiety or shame. Doing the right thing may make you feel terrible because you have become so accustomed to doing the wrong thing. We can't judge what is right by feelings, even though I have often heard Christians give this advice. Quoting Colossians 3:15, "Let the peace of Christ rule in your hearts," people tell us we can know the will of God if, after making a decision, we have peace. However, the context of this verse, which is about unity with other Christians, does not permit this general application. Christians cannot always trust their feelings and their consciences to signal God's will, as we will see more clearly in another chapter. We must risk doing wrong if we are going to risk doing right.

Many of the most daring risks will come as we try to relate to our parents, whether they are living or not. Our next two resolves are about that.

Notes

1. Wilson, pp. 59-60.

2. Ellen Bass and Louise Thornton, eds., *I Never Told Anyone* (New York: Harper & Row Publishers, 1983), p. 90.

3. *The Twelve Steps for Adult Children* (San Diego: Recovery Publications, 1987), p. 51.

RESOLVE

No longer avoiding any anger
we may feel toward our parents,
we will deal with it, along with
the issue of forgiving them.

6

Considering Forgiveness

"I can never forgive him; he's the most insensitive person you will ever meet. He doesn't care about me. After what he's done to me, I don't care if I ever see him again." Louise spoke of her father. She was unhappy and depressed, and her marriage was in trouble. She constantly criticized her husband and was afraid she would lose her temper and hurt her baby girl.

Could Louise's hatred for her dad be spilling into her marriage? Was she scorching her husband with angry outbursts because of wrath toward her dad? Would her depression go away if her anger did not? Must she forgive her father to be free from her past?

Anger and resentment are two powerful emotions experienced by those dealing with the hurt of their childhood homes. The adult child's feelings toward his parents are usually bittersweet, often a mixture of warm love and intense hatred. Our support group found that some of us repressed our love for our parents, while some of us stuffed our anger. It's unhealthy to do either.

If the bitter taste of your family life makes you insensitive to the good in your parents, you are not only being unfair to them, but to yourself. We can't divorce our parents; we are always their child, and how we think about them will determine in part how we think about ourselves. To get a proper perspective of ourselves we must work on a true perspective of them.

Sometimes we can be so absorbed in our bitterness that we don't take charge of our own lives. We have to get beyond blaming our parents. On the other hand, not tasting the bitter because of the sweet may be just as dangerous. Nine-year-old Darlwin Carlisle shows how deep is the affection of children for parents. In Gary, Indiana, January 1988, Darlwin's mother left her in the attic bedroom of an unheated house. A refrigerator barricaded the door. Two days later authorities found her dehydrated and severely frostbitten. From the hospital where doctors had amputated both of Darlwin's legs, reporters wrote: "What [Darlwin] asked for over and over was to see her mother." That was impossible. Her mother was in jail.[1]

Children bandage the wounds inflicted by their parents in wrappings of natural love. A large part of recovery involves taking off the false bandages and looking at the raw wounds. When they do this, some get genuinely angry with their parents for the first time. One day Darlwin will have to deal with her conflicting feelings toward her mother and look openly at the damage done to her.

WHEN IT'S TOUGH TO FORGIVE

Bitter, hurt, and confused, many adult children ask, "Must I forgive my parents to be free from my past?" Janet, a Christian woman in her late thirties, slips out quietly after the church service. Facing people is so difficult. She has never married because she fears intimacy; she has financial problems because she leaves a job when people start to get close. In an interview she explains:

My father began to rape me when I was five years old. It continued on a regular basis until my late teens. My mother knew about it and told me it was all right for him to do it. I wanted it to stop but I was afraid to tell anyone. Once, in junior high, I confided in a teacher who had befriended me. The principal called my father into his office to talk with him and the teacher about it. My father convinced them I was lying. When he got home from the meeting he beat me with a hammer; when they took me to the hospital with my battered face, broken jaw, and numerous concussions, they told the authorities I had fallen from a window. I never told anyone again until I left home.

When the family secret was finally told, the father was sent to prison for his crimes. Forgiveness doesn't easily flow from the hearts of people like Janet. They raise questions about forgiveness that aren't always asked by those whose afflictions seem trivial by comparison—questions like,

Isn't it sometimes all right not to forgive . . . don't I have a right to be angry?

Didn't Jesus say to the Apostles, "If you forgive anyone his sins, they are forgiven; **if you do not forgive them, they are not forgiven**"? (John 20:23, emphasis mine)

Does forgiving mean that I should never be angry with my parents for what they have done?

Should I forgive my parents if they show no evidence of repentance?

If I do forgive, will I instantly feel good toward my parents? If I don't, does that mean I haven't really forgiven them?

Does forgiving mean I must now act toward my parents as if nothing ever happened? Must I trust them?

What should I do if my parent is continuing to abuse my sister like he did me?

In this chapter and the next, I want to try to deal with these questions. I want to show that the process isn't always simple and that the victim doesn't always bear the whole burden of forgiving. I want to show that forgiveness is sometimes conditional; if certain conditions are not met, forgiveness is not extended until they are. I want to show how not forgiving may be a way of getting rid of the bitterness toward someone who has sinned against you.

A BIBLICAL VIEW OF FORGIVENESS

The New Testament view of forgiveness includes the following elements: (1) Forgiveness is demanded only when one is sinned against. Today we use the word more broadly; we forgive a person's mistake or forgive him for accidentally stepping on our toes. In the New Testament, you don't really forgive someone's mistakes; you forbear them. You don't forgive someone with whom you have a personality clash; you tolerate them. (2) Forgiveness means letting go of any debt the person owes you, giving up any attempt to retaliate for the harm they have done to you. Forgiveness is surrendering our right to get even. (3) Forgiveness means letting go of resentment. When we forgive, we refuse to punish the offender with our bitter attitude. (4) Human forgiveness is sometimes connected to God's forgiveness. That doesn't only mean that when God forgives we ought to forgive, but also that when we forgive, God forgives. For this reason, we ought to be careful how and when we forgive someone, because by doing so the person is made to feel God has also forgiven them (see 2 Corinthians 2:5-8).

At times there is no connection between human and divine forgiveness, such as when an unbeliever seeks our forgiveness but doesn't ask God for His. In these cases, we forgive but God doesn't. Let's look at forgiveness and nonforgiveness more closely.

FROM BITTER TO BETTER

Bitterness Burns

Let's start with something that almost everyone agrees on: Animosity toward your parents is bad, for you and for them. Anger, like a campfire, becomes dangerous in two ways. We can fan it into a roaring blaze that ignites the trees around it, or we can ignore it while it quietly extends fiery fingers into the forest. Some adult children are unaware of the angry, smoldering embers that singe them and those who get too near.

Bitterness does burn. It does horrible, devastating things inside our soul. Anger is like a fluid that builds up in our inner psychic storage tank: If it gets too full, it breaks out in terrible ways. It can turn on the innocent, or we can turn it on ourselves. If it doesn't escape somehow, the pressure can inflict internal damage—high blood pressure, migraine headaches, ulcers, diarrhea, constipation, or worse.[2]

Many Christian authors sound the same warning. David Augsburger claims unforgiving resentment is like a bulldog that clenches the teeth of memory into the past and refuses to let go.[3] Lewis Smedes believes that it hurts more to not forgive than to forgive. "Revenge glues us to the past," he writes," and it dooms us to repeat it."[4] Richard Walters makes a stronger statement: "When we don't forgive, life is like being alone in a deep hole. Our freedom is gone. By day we see the sun overhead, hear the talk and laughter of others as they enjoy life, and know that we are missing out on the joy of living that we should have. By night we sit huddled, lonely and fearful, in the bottom of this pit, angry at ourselves for having dug the pit and for having stepped into it through our failure to forgive. Resentment begins to control our lives. Forgiving is the only cure for resentment."[5]

The Bible speaks graphically about the destructiveness of bitterness: "Make every effort to live in peace with all men. . . . See to it that no one misses the grace of God and that no bitter root grows up to cause trouble and defile many" (Hebrews 12:14, 15). The apostle Paul is quite blunt: "Get rid of all bitterness, rage and anger . . . along with every form of malice" (Ephesians 4:31).

Yet the question remains: Must we forgive in order to rid ourselves of anger and bitterness? Everyone I studied said yes. But if this were the only point to be made, you'd have to feel trapped. Someone has victimized you; if you are revengeful and resentful, you destroy yourself. Never mind the offender goes free; you must free yourself. You now feel you are three times a victim: of abuse, of your own anger toward the abuser, and of those who insist you simply drop the matter before it drops you. There is more to Christian forgiveness than that. It isn't just—slam-bang—you sinned, I forgive. Scripture lays down a series of steps for us to follow.

Step One: Acknowledge the Sin

The process begins when a Christian sins against you. "If your brother sins against you, go and show him his fault, just between the two of you. If he listens to you, you have won your brother over" (Matthew 18:15). If someone has wronged us, we are to go to that person and confront him or her about it.

We can't just walk away from our dysfunctional homes. Yet many counselors suggest we keep our resentments to ourselves and not talk to our parents about them. If they are talking about our parents' mistakes, failures, and shortcomings, I would agree. But if our parents sinned against us, we need to recognize it happened, and they need to be told about it. We not only do it for our sakes, but for theirs; we want to give them a chance to repent and to be forgiven.

Step Two: Recognize the Indignation

Recognizing you have been sinned against includes the right to be indignant about it. Nothing in the Bible prohibits anger in such situations. Granted, Scripture frequently condemns anger, and being angry could be as bad as committing murder: "You have heard that it was said to the people long ago, `Do not murder, and anyone who murders will be subject to judgment.' But I tell you that anyone who is angry with his brother will be subject to judgment. Again, anyone who says to his brother, `Raca,' (a term of contempt) is answerable to the Sanhedrin. But anyone who says `You fool!' will be in danger of the fire of hell" (Matthew 5:21-22). But anger is sometimes okay: " `In your anger do not sin.' Do not let the sun go down while you are still angry," said the apostle Paul (Ephesians 4:26). Anger or indignation is an emotion we feel when we have been victimized. When we feel it, we should do something about it. We should not allow it to continue unresolved.

Anger's Assets

Quick forgiveness skips the anger and often ignores the sin. Anger is something like pain; it's a signal that something is wrong. We won't get rid of pain by simply wishing it away. We relieve it by doing something about the problem. The same is true of righteous anger; we dissolve it by facing the problem. It may be a serious mistake to think that we can be deeply wronged and simply shake off our emotional responses.

Many adult children are like the middle-aged man who recently told me:

I thought I had no anger left for my mother, that I had forgiven her for what she had done to me. As a loving Christian, I thought I had forgiven her many years ago. But when I started to deal with some of my personal problems and saw how ashamed I really was of how she left my father and dragged me around while she slept with one man after another, I got very angry. I didn't know it was in me.

Just the other day I asked one of our students, an ACoA, how he was doing. "I'm getting in touch with my anger," he said.

"Do you mean the anger you had as a child, or the anger you feel now, realizing the effect of your alcoholic home?"

"A little of both," he said. "But, mostly, I'm recognizing the anger I felt as a child and am trying to deal with it."

"Didn't you feel anger at your father when you were a child?"

"Oh, yes, I did. But I didn't really handle it. I didn't tell him. I didn't lash out at him. I felt angry and virtually ignored it."

The first step in dealing with anger is to admit it and recognize you have a right to it. Often in our group meetings someone admits being mad at a parent and someone else counsels: "Let go of it." But that advice ignores the fact that you can't let go of what you don't have hold of. It's especially tough to get a grip on what you feel about your parents because your natural love for them inhibits feelings of anger. Charles Whitfield reminds us of the kinds of statements we use to protect our parents. We deny: "My childhood was just fine." We fantasize: "It really didn't happen that way." Or we fear rejection or punishment: "If I express my rage, they won't love me; something bad will happen." We might even attack those who point out our parent's shortcomings: "You're bad for suggesting that . . . my parents could not have been bad." We are taught that parents are to be held in honor, not contempt; they are to be respected, not rebuked. Those attitudes make it hard to forgive their sin because it's hard to acknowledge their sin.

It takes courage to admit anger, especially when you're a child. It's even scarier to show it. The parent is bigger, more powerful, and someone you should love.

A woman in our group said she had just written a letter to her mother describing how much she loved her and that everything was fine between them. Then she said how disappointed she was in herself because she had lied. Things were not fine between her and her mother, who was nigh impossible to live with and certainly impossible to please. Her sharp criticism and unreasonable demands ruined holidays and upset countless evenings. She was never certain when her mother's outbursts would terrorize the household. "When Dad came home at night, before facing Mom, he would take one of us aside to ask, `Is your mother all right this evening?' " This young woman placed the same unmerciful demands on herself, her husband, and her child. Her drive to have everything just right was sapping the joy out of her life and her family's. She was angry, but she had a terrible time believing she had been wronged. This pattern was learned in childhood: After a tirade and the resulting dismal evening or holiday, her mother would plead for assurance that she really hadn't ruined things. And the daughter would always give in. Giving in is not forgiving. To forgive, we must recognize a wrong has been done. To forgive, we must permit ourselves some anger, some righteous indignation.

I agree with Rachael V., who edited a book of the personal stories of abused women: "If you jump into forgiveness without experiencing the anger and grief, then that forgiveness isn't going to be genuine. It takes time, and there are stages you have to go through to get to forgiveness. Forgiveness is the goal, for sure, but it takes some real work to get there."[6] Denying the wrong by denying anger is the heart of the problem for dysfunctional homes. Denying the problem perpetuates it. Offering forgiveness before the offender admits his wrong does little good for anyone.

Recently, when an Iraqi pilot fired a missile into a U.S. ship, killing thirty-seven crew members, the family of one of the victims told the pilot, "We forgive you." Isn't this overlooking the crime? Overlooking the harm too quickly confuses both the person sinned against and the person who has sinned. This is especially painful for children of dysfunctional families, already confused by a lifetime of whitewashing. They have learned to put up with all kinds of gross ill-treatment and even feel guilty for not being more tolerant. Frequently they let people walk all over them.

Not Allowed to Feel Wronged

A survey of the books and articles dealing with forgiveness of parents shows how misleading well-meaning people can be. When urging adults to forgive their parents, their advice usually supports the following myths.

Myth #1: *Our parents meant no harm.* "All parents want to do what is best for their children," claims one author. This is hard to swallow for someone who at twelve years of age was blamed for her dad's drinking, or a boy whose father abandoned him when he was eight years of age, or someone who bears the scars of his mother's beatings. Parents are sometimes selfish, unloving, sinful. When they wrong their children, good intentions do not turn that wrong into right. We Christians do not ask God to forgive us for our trespasses because "we were only trying to do what was best." Forgiveness is necessary because wrongs have been committed.

Myth #2. *Parents were unable to do better because of their own upbringing.* Sometimes this rings true; we recognize our parents' own childhoods may have handicapped them. But it doesn't provide a basis for forgiveness. You don't mask failure by the term *unable.* No one should ever tell herself she is "unable" to show love. Failing to show love is wrong; it is even more wrong when we claim there is nothing we can do about it. We must not blame our sins on our moms and dads, nor should we permit them to blame theirs on our grandparents.

Myth #3: *Parents didn't realize what they were doing.* In discussions on forgiveness, Jesus is often quoted: "Father, forgive them; for they know not what they do." But Jesus' prayer was not uttered because they were unaware of their sin in executing an innocent man; Jesus asked forgiveness for them because they didn't know they were putting to death the Son of God.

Is a father to be forgiven for repeatedly raping his daughter because he really doesn't know what sexual abuse does to a woman? "It won't hurt anyone" is what we tell ourselves when we justify something God tells us is wrong. The alcoholic who puts his family under severe stress isn't entirely blind to the suffering he causes; he just makes himself blind. Even after years of punishing their families I have heard alcoholics say, "The only person I hurt was myself." Do such people really not know what they are doing? We must distinguish ignorance of sin from ignorance of its consequences.

Myth # 4: *We should forgive our parents because they were sick*. The mentally and physically ill are not always responsible for what they do. They don't need forgiveness, they need patience and understanding.

The hurt inflicted by an addicted or abusive parent, however, makes the sickness question more complicated. Experts don't agree on whether alcoholics are ill. The American Medical Association labels alcoholism a disease because its traits are similar to one. Alcoholics, like sick persons, can't seem to control themselves. Probably the best definition for an alcoholic is the one provided by the National Council on Alcoholism: "The person with alcoholism cannot consistently predict on any drinking occasion the duration of the episode or the quantity that will be consumed."[7] Alcoholism progresses like a sickness; if left untreated, it will progress with certain symptoms that lead to mental damage, physical incapacity, and premature death. In most cases, but not all, the alcoholic's brain eventually fails to function normally. Some add a third feature of the disease: denial. Unlike other illnesses which warn of disease through symptoms of pain or fatigue, alcoholism signals the sufferer that everything is just dandy; no problem.

While abundant evidence confirms the first two features of alcoholism, the third isn't so certain. When someone denies a problem that wrecks a marriage, rouses a daughter's hate, totals two cars in traffic accidents, isn't that denial a moral wrong? And is this denial so unique? Don't workaholics, foodaholics, and those with other personal problems also deny them?

As a Christian, I have trouble blaming a disease for blinding a person to the pain and wreckage he or she creates. I'll blame the sinful nature for that. Whether we are alcoholics or not, the road to recovery starts with admitting that we need to be rescued. "If we confess our sins, he is faithful and just to forgive us our sins and to cleanse us from all unrighteousness." In the original language, the word *confess* literally means "to say the same thing." In confession we stop lying and we face the truth about ourselves. That's repentance. I cannot call the inability to repent a sickness, unless I call the sickness "sin." Alcoholics are ethically responsible, not because they can't stop drinking, but because they won't admit they can't.

The popular notion that when an alcoholic says he has a disease, he or she is claiming no responsibility for the drinking and the damage it causes is not true. Those who claim it's a disease believe the alcoholic owes it to himself and others to seek a cure. Calling his or her problem a disease doesn't change that. In fact, it encourages the average problem drinker to seek treatment. The alcoholic is relieved to learn that he or she is sick, not just wicked and weak.

Not admitting to a problem makes an alcoholic or any other addict culpable for the pain they afflict on others. Part of the recovery of those in the Alcoholics Anonymous program includes making a list of people they have harmed and making amends. They are as forgivable as anyone else, but not because of any so-called illness.

The victims of addicted and abusive parents have a right to be indignant and angry, yet patient when waiting for admission of wrongdoing. The addict is tortured by guilt within, and even when he recognizes his problem and begins to recover, the guilt is so overwhelming he has a hard time looking at the damage he's caused. It may take several years for an alcoholic to return to normal thinking. Recovering alcoholics and abusers will need our love and patience. It may take a long time before we hear them say a sincere "I'm sorry."

Myth #5. *We should be willing to forgive because we are partly to blame.* David Augsburger writes, "How does one deal with the pain, anger and injustice felt when wronged by another? First, by reducing the sense of outraged innocence. When angry, most human beings prefer to see the other as the invader, attacker, exploiter, and the self as the innocent victim. Maintaining this definition frees the self from blame and responsibility while laying it solely at the other's doorstep. However, such one-sided injustices are rare among continuing relationships."[8] While Augsburger is correct in saying both parties are often responsible for a wrong between them, his statement could perpetuate the plight of the true victims, who have already taken much of the blame for what happened in their family; parents often heaped it upon them. To suggest that one-sided injustices are rare will only make victims wallow in needless guilt.

Myth #6: *Parents should be forgiven because they should be honored.* This argument is most troublesome to adult children because they get all churned up when they try to mix honor and anger. One girl expressed it well: *Pondering my past makes me so angry with my mother. Now, I have a hard time loving her. This is just the opposite of before. Then, I loved her and had a hard time being angry with her.* In time, she will be able to handle both emotions at once because there is no reason why we can't honor and love a person at the same time we are angry with him or her.

In Scripture, to honor your parents meant primarily three things: 1) to obey them; 2) to respect their teaching; 3) to care for them in their old age. Interestingly, there is no specific command anywhere to love your parents. But if we honor our parents, we should give them every benefit of the doubt, try to see their good sides, appreciate all they have done for us, and be willing to care for them when they are helpless. We can do all of those things and be upset with them for wrongs they have done. We can still see their faults and their sins, and possibly refuse to forgive them.

Step Three: Be Willing to Forgive

When Jesus told us to go to an offending brother and "show him his fault," he was not suggesting an act of vengeance. Actually, he was proposing an act of love. To do so requires a willingness to forgive since you are obligated to do so if the person repents (Luke 17:3). This eagerness to forgive is one of the highest Christian virtues. It is the essence of Paul's plea: "Be kind and compassionate to one another, forgiving each other, just as in Christ God forgave you." It is the driving force behind the parable of the unmerciful servant. Relieved by his master of a debt of millions of dollars, this servant found one of his fellow servants who owed him a few dollars. He grabbed him and began to choke him. "Pay back what you owe me!" he demanded. When he refused to pay back the few dollars, the servant who was forgiven millions sent the man to prison. When the master heard about it, he called the servant in. "You wicked servant," he said, "I canceled all that debt of yours because you begged me to. Shouldn't you have had mercy on your fellow servant just as I had on you?" (Matthew 18:21-35).

Christians are willing to forgive others because God has forgiven them. Corrie ten Boom tells of how she was able to forgive atrocious wrongs for just this reason. Having survived the years of Nazi cruelty which had taken the lives of her family, she preached forgiveness in Europe and the United States. Lewis Smedes describes her reaction after a sermon she had preached in Munich. A man come toward her, hand outstretched. "Ja, fraulein, it is wonderful that Jesus forgives us all our sins, just as you say." She remembered his face; it was the leering, lecherous, mocking face of one of the SS guards. Her hand froze at her side. She could not forgive. She thought she had forgiven all. But she could not forgive when she met a guard, standing in the solid flesh in front of her. Ashamed, horrified at herself, she prayed, "Lord, forgive me, I cannot forgive." And as she prayed she felt forgiven, accepted, in spite of her shabby performance as a famous forgiver. Her hand was suddenly unfrozen. The ice of hate melted. Her hand went out. She forgave as she felt forgiven."[9]

The foundation for forgiveness is the cross of Jesus Christ. We can forgive, not because our parents were sick, had good intentions, or didn't know what they were doing. We forgive because we ourselves have been forgiven for our selfishness and sin. Forgiven, we forgive.

Step Four: Confront the Offender

Willingness to forgive is not the same as forgiving. When we as Christians aim to forgive as Christ has forgiven us we are compelled to take the next step: to confront our parent. "Show him his fault, just between the two of you," said Jesus. Could it be that some people don't confront because they don't want to forgive?

Rarely do books about forgiveness mention this step. One book on dealing with parents even suggests we should write lists of resentments we have toward our parents, meditate on them, and burn them. This may be necessary if our parents are not living or if they have already refused to listen to us.

When we forgive without rebuking, however, we do little good for the one who sinned against us. Knowing about the damage gives him a chance to do what Jesus said he should do: "If he listens to you, you have won your brother over" (Matthew 18:15).

Step Five: The Offender Repents

To listen is to repent, according to Luke 17:3. "If your brother sins rebuke him, and if he repents, forgive him." We should be generous with our mercy when there is repentance. "If he sins against you seven times in a day, and seven times comes back to you and says, `I repent,' forgive him."

These New Testament verses don't explain specifically what repentance means. In the Old Testament, repentance was usually a public act. It required going to the temple to present a sin offering. Repentance means more than saying you are sorry. Alcoholics often mutter their apologies at the very moment they are making plans for their next binge. Addicts' and abusers' remorseful promises to "never do it again" should not be confused with true repentance. People who truly repent will admit to having a problem and take steps toward solving it. When we continue to accept less from them, we participate in their lack of repentance and perpetuate the problem. We also confuse the issue of sin.

Confronting Makes Letting Go Easier

Confrontation is one of the best ways to let go of bitterness. Too often people hold on to resentment because the wrong has never been dealt with. When someone sins, is rebuked, and truly repents, truth is declared. If we secretly, silently try to forgive people who have grossly wronged us, we get more confused about right and wrong. We have a need to distinguish between normal and abnormal, just and unjust. To simply write off wrong actions brutalizes our sense of justice.

When parents victimize their children and then admit it, children learn the truth about themselves. Parents' failure to own up to their abuse or neglect leaves children with deep bitterness, which they hold onto in order to hold onto reality.

In our group meetings, hurt people tell their stories again and again, as if to attempt to shock us into agreeing terrible things were done to them. "Regularly I would come home and find my mother on the couch with a strange man, yet she called *me* a slut," a woman tells us once again, wanting us to nod our heads and confirm once again she was wronged. She is afraid to confront her mother, and her resentful retelling of the past is a way of assuring herself of the truth of her past.

I realize that sometimes we hold on to our resentments to feel superior to others or to punish them. One writer says that we keep our resentment to maintain power over people or to serve our self-righteousness.[10] Yet an adult child might be mad simply because he is looking for justice. We want people to be fair with us; we want people to admit we've been wronged. When people fail to confirm we were victims, they fail to recognize injustice. This infuriates us. Flippant advice to forgive and forget merely stokes the fires of resentment.

Step Six: Forgive the Offender

Once the offender repents, there is no need for the offended to cling to the past in order to cling to the truth. Smedes writes, "To forgive is to put down your 50-pound pack after a 10-mile climb up a mountain. . . . To forgive is to set a prisoner free and discover the prisoner was you. To forgive is to reach back into your hurting past and recreate it in your memory so that you can begin again. . . . To forgive is to dance to the beat of God's forgiving heart. It is to ride the tide of love's strongest wave. Our only escape from history's cruel unfairness, our only passage to the future's creative possibilities, is the miracle of forgiving."[11]

Debbie, a friend, told me of a confrontation that broke down the wall between her father and her. She was the subject of a magazine article on the effects of divorce on teens. "*As I was growing up at home, my father never laughed, never hugged me, and only once said he loved me. That was on my sixteenth birthday—the same day he told me he was leaving home. I was never close to my father, but then nobody was. He once admitted to Mom that he has a wall built around himself, and that if anybody comes too close, it shakes the bricks.*" This made her write words to him she dare not say or let him read: "*Father, I wish you knew I feel I'm missing some important part of my personality because of your rejection of me. Even though we shared the same house for sixteen years, I felt like I was living in a glass booth, cut off from what love and affection you might have offered. Others see me as a pretty normal, happy seventeen-year-old senior. But when I look in the mirror and think of you, I feel an aching sense of loneliness that eats at my insides like a tapeworm.*" Besides her longing to be loved by her father, Debbie felt frustrated and angry.

They rarely saw each other and he made no effort to show her any love. After several years, she decided she would not wait for him to make the first move. She sketched a picture of him, phoned to arrange a meeting to give it to him, and wrote to him once again words not intended for his eyes: "*Father, I wish you knew how scared I am to stick out my neck like this and love you first. I'm scared you might reject what little I have to give. Even though I am a young woman now, almost grown in your eyes, I still have the ceramic heart of a little girl. So, Father, if I call you Daddy when I give you this picture, if I jump into your arms and squeeze your neck and cry, please don't laugh. Hug me back, Daddy, hug me back.*" There was no breakthrough when she gave him the picture, but it had seemed to help.

The turning point she hoped for came after her father read the magazine article, something she had tried to prevent. Since no names appeared in it, he would never have known it spoke of him, except that someone pointed it out to him. Debbie feared their next meeting. But he shocked her by saying, "All you said is true. I'm sorry." Finally they talked about his feelings and their relationship. "Now, my dad and I talk all the time about him and me and all kinds of things," she says with deep satisfaction.

Many of our adult children tell how difficult it is to forgive even when their parent is remorseful. "I still hate to be in the same room with my father," said one of the members of our group. "Even though he is depressed about the past, has tearfully agonized over his failures as a father, even though he is undergoing treatment for his addictions to drugs and alcohol, I have a terrible time forgiving him for what he has been." In the last step in this chapter, we will deal with this struggle to forgive. Before that, let's see what we should do if the offender doesn't repent.

Alternate Step Five: Take Along One or Two Witnesses

What can be done when the Christian offender is confronted and refuses to admit his wrong? Jesus tells us: "But if he will not listen, take one or two others along, so that `every matter may be established by the testimony of two or three witnesses,' " (Matthew 18:16). This visit is an expression of love. Others are there to confirm to the person that he has sinned. Today this is a standard approach to abusers and addicts. In another chapter, I'll spell out the steps for you, in case one or both of your parents need such an "intervention."

Christian adult children should seek the help of other Christians when confronting Christian parents who refuse to own up to abuse.

Alternate Step Six: Take the Matter to the Church

If the offender continues to be stubborn, Jesus instructs us to "tell it to the church," (Matthew 18:17). The apostle

Paul gave similar instructions. Disputes between Christians were not to be glibly forgotten but taken to the church for judgment (1 Corinthians 6:1-8). This is a difficult step because not all parents are Christians and church members, and not all churches are in the habit of handling disputes in this way. Yet an adult child can try to enlist the help of the church board, particularly when the abuse has been severe and if brothers or sisters are currently threatened. Pastors are obligated by law to take such cases to the authorities if they know about them.

More and more the church is forced to deal with such situations. Several churches I know have disciplined men who have sexually abused their daughters. One of our faculty members described how a young woman revealed to him that her father, a minister, had sexually abused her. Besides counseling with her, he confronted the father, who was unwilling to deal with his problem. Eventually, the father was disciplined by his church and dismissed from his pastorate. Such drastic action is in keeping with the words of Jesus.

Alternate Step Seven: Dismiss the Person from the Church

The church sometimes has to be tough. "If he refuses to listen even to the church, treat him as you would a pagan or a tax collector," said Jesus (Matthew 18:17). Even though Jesus warned us that God would forgive us our debts as we would forgive our debtors, He taught that it was sometimes right not to forgive (Matthew 6:12, 14, 15; John 20:23). This is because our forgiveness is conditional, as is God's. When the church has pointed out someone's sin and he or she has not listened, the church does not forgive. It is a signal to the sinner that God also has not forgiven, explained Jesus. "I tell you the truth, whatever you bind on earth will be bound in heaven, and whatever you loose on earth will be loosed in heaven" (Matthew 18:18).

Refusing to forgive will not permit the offender to wallow in his denial unchallenged. Unconditional love does not require unconditional forgiveness. In this case, unforgiveness is an act of love. The dismissal is without bitterness. This is not a matter of holding a grudge, but of holding onto the truth. The congregation stands willing to forgive when the person acknowledges his guilt.

It is difficult to know what the offended person does in this case. He or she is under no obligation to forgive in the sense of letting the person "off the hook." Yet the offended one ought to let go of any bitterness. The congregation has made that easier by their support. A victim will have less pressure to cling to resentment, since the injustice has been publicly recognized and he or she is cleared of any doubt of wrong. The offended one is supported and affirmed.

When there is no genuine repentance on the part of the victimizer, the church's not forgiving is one way a victim gains self-respect.

QUESTIONS ABOUT FORGIVING

When the offender repents we are obligated to forgive without limit. When Peter asked Jesus the question, "Lord, how many times shall I forgive my brother when he sins against me? Up to seven times?" Jesus answered: "I tell you, not seven times, but seventy-seven times" (Matthew 18:21-22).

Even after deciding not to retaliate against someone, we still have some practical issues to deal with. The words of a young woman display the typical confusion of adult children. *"I try to forgive my parents. I often pray for it. But sometimes it seems that old things come up and I can't forget and think I didn't really forgive. But I know that I should forgive them and I'm still working on it."* What does it mean to forgive "from the heart," as Jesus taught in Matthew 18:35? Do sour feelings toward parents instantly dissolve? Do you have to forget to forgive? How do you treat the person afterwards? Do you act like nothing ever happened?

Must We Feel Forgiveness?

These forgiveness questions terrorized a woman I once counseled. Her deep depression and threats of suicide prompted her husband to ask me to see her. In despair, she explained that she was no longer sure she was a born-again Christian. "If I were," she said softly, her shoulders and head sagging in torment, "I could forgive." She had been hurt badly in a longlasting conflict with a person who had since come to apologize. "I still can't forgive her," she said.

"Forgiveness means you will give up any plans to retaliate," I said. "Do you plan to harm this woman?"

"Oh, no," she quickly replied.

"Do you pray for her to be punished?"

"Certainly not."

"Will you gossip about and defame this person in an attempt to get even?"

"No."

"Will you not refuse to speak to this woman and when you see her will you try to treat her like anyone else?"

"Yes."

"Then, it sounds to me like you have forgiven her."

"Jesus has given me no such feeling," the woman said, staring at the floor.

I agreed that we should cast our bitterness on the great forgiver, Jesus Christ, and trust Him for love, but at the same time I tried to explain that resentment is not always so easily discarded. We should not always expect so much of ourselves. Sometimes it takes awhile for our feelings of forgiveness to catch up with our decision to forgive. Wounds may be deep, inflicted over many years. Surely God, who commanded us to forgive from the heart, will enable us to do so. But after we have forgiven with our will and prayed, we must wait for Him to deal with our feelings. Even after we have felt warmth toward someone who has wronged us, the resentment may reappear.

We need to give our emotions time to catch up with our actions. Animosity that took time to build may sometimes require time to be torn down. Ray, emotionally battered by his father for eighteen years, told us he was now able to say "I love you" to his dad, though it was still difficult to be in the same room with him. Our group didn't blame Ray for harboring leftover negative feelings toward his father, nor did we complain to God for not removing them. We thanked God and applauded Ray for progress in what may still be a long process.

Must We Forget?

Another unreasonable demand we sometimes make of ourselves is thinking we must forget in order to forgive. The idea comes from Scripture about God's forgiving us: "I, even I, am he who blots out your transgressions, for my own sake, and remembers your sins no more" (Isaiah 43:25). Did He not promise Israel, "As far as the east is from the west, so far has he removed our transgressions from us" (Psalm 103:12). Should we not forgive and forget, as God does?

To answer this we must first see that God doesn't really forget. Though these passages of Scripture seem to suggest that He does, it is clear from other parts of the Bible that He still remembers. God's people, Israel, were forgiven for their rebellion after God led them out of Egypt (Numbers 14:19). Yet, speaking later on behalf of

God, Moses cautions them, "Never forget how you provoked the LORD your God to anger in the desert" (Deuteronomy 9:7). Other portions of Scripture show how God not only remembers past sins, but asks His people to remember (Ezekiel 16:1-8; 1 Corinthians 6:11; Ephesians 2:1-3). There is no contradiction as long as we understand what God's "forgetting" truly means. It does not mean that God has no memory of them. If so, God would have to ignore the Scriptures, since they record in detail countless stories of forgiven sins. Forgetting is a metaphor that means God will not judge us for forgiven sins; they are as good as forgotten.

Forgiving others means that we will not do or say anything to get even or show resentment for the wrongs done to us. It also means that we try to put them behind us and not recall them whenever we see the offender. It means that we hope eventually to remember them for the good things and good times. But it is impossible to forget the past.

Do I Act As If Nothing Ever Happened?

Forgiveness may not even mean acting entirely as if the wrong never took place. J. Oliver Buswell, an evangelical theologian prominent a few decades ago, pointed this out in a story. Buswell said we should forgive as Christ forgave us. But he was realistic. During a testimony time at a prayer meeting focusing on forgiveness, a carpenter stood with tears in his eyes and asked for advice. Some years before, he climbed onto a scaffolding that had been poorly constructed by another carpenter. It collapsed, throwing the man to the floor and sending him to the hospital with serious injuries. After weeks of recovery, the carpenter returned to work. "Now," said the man, "I do not feel bitterness in my heart toward that man and if I could do him good in any way, I should certainly do so. But I cannot bring myself to step onto a scaffolding built by that man without examining it and testing its security. I want to ask you Christian brethren if in your judgment I am cherishing unforgiveness?" Buswell writes: "Of course, the unanimous answer was in the negative."[12]

This makes sense. If someone has deceived, betrayed, or failed us, it won't be as easy to trust them as if they had never done so. "Even though I have forgiven my parents, being with them is still awkward and difficult," is a common statement from adult children, whose relationship with the parents needs a lot of repair. Sometimes they have to do the work alone because the parents are unrepentant, uncooperative, or dead. Yet it's possible to make peace with parents, with or without their help. The next chapter suggests how.

Notes

1. Nancy Ryan and Rob Karwath, "Gary Girl Loses Legs, Still Filled with Love," *Chicago Tribune*, January 22, 1988, sec. 1, p. 1.

2. Carol Travis, *Anger: The Misunderstood Emotion* (New York: Simon and Schuster, 1982), pp. 95, 96.

3. David Augsburger, *Caring Enough to Forgive* (Ventura, Ca.: Regal Books, 1981), pp. 12-13.

4. Lewis B. Smedes, "Forgiveness: The Power to Change the Past," *Christianity Today*, January 7, 1983, p. 26.

5. Richard P. Walters, *Forgive and Be Free* (Grand Rapids: Zondervan Publishing House, 1983), p. 16.

6. Rachel V., *Family Secrets: Life Stories of Adult Children of Alcoholics* (San Francisco: (Harper & Row, Publishers, 1987), p. 22.

7. *Annals of Internal Medicine* 85 (1976):764.

8. Augsburger, p. 10.

9. Smedes, p. 26.

10. John Patton and Brian H. Childs, *Christian Marriage and Family* (Nashville: Abingdon Press, 1988), pp. 167-68.

11. Smedes, p. 26.

12. J. Oliver Buswell, *A Systematic Theology of the Christian Religion* (Grand Rapids: Zondervan Publishing Co., 1962), Vol. II, p. 131.

RESOLVE

We will resolve any bitterness
we feel toward our parents,
whether living or dead,
and seek to relate to them
or our memory of them ,
in positive ways.

7

Dealing with
Parents

B reaking the bitterness bondage to your parents begins with coming to terms with these feelings. We have seen how the biblical process of forgiveness can help set us free from them. Yet bitter feelings can linger even after your parent has truly repented and you have forgiven, especially if your parent isn't remorseful or helpful in bridging the gap between you. Many adult children still battle hard feelings toward parents who are dead. Whether living or dead, there are things we can do to make peace with our parents in our hearts and, when possible, in our relationships.

IDENTIFY THE RESENTMENTS

Start by making an inventory of your resentments. This suggestion may look strange to some adult children who know full well why they are angry with their parents. But sometimes the reasons for our animosity lie below the surface of our consciousness. This undefined emotional blob becomes a monster that invades other areas of our lives, making us resentful of life itself and even bitter toward God. Because we don't focus clearly on the reasons for our resentments, we don't get a complete picture of our parents, and we overlook the positive traits that could make respecting them easier. Statements adult children make show how dark feelings toward their parents eclipse the good. "My dad was respected in the community; ha, ha; what people didn't know was that instead of devoting his evenings to his family, he devoted them to beer and whiskey; he ended each day in a drunken stupor. I can't help but hate him."

In his helpful book, *Making Peace with Your Parents*, Harold H. Bloomfield calls this distorted picture of a parent an **inner parent**. He claims, "The first step in making peace with your parents is to make peace with your inner parents."[1] He offers a powerful and practical technique for doing this. For some adult children, this exercise is like surgery; it could be so painful that they shouldn't try it unless they are in the care of a competent counselor.

Bloomfield's exercise consists of using paper and pen to bring hidden resentments out into the open where you can deal with them. Make a list of everything you can think of that caused any animosity you may feel toward your parents. Be specific. Avoid generalizations like, "I hate my father." Instead, list details about what caused your hatred. Bloomfield offers some examples of how someone might write about an abusive mother:

"I resent that you slapped me at school in the first grade in front of my friends."

"I resent feeling like you never wanted me to be born."

"I resent how you make it seem like I am to blame for your unhappiness," etc.

While drafting this list, which may fill scores of pages, you'll no doubt experience a flood of feelings, which is the purpose for doing it. Let them happen, and freely cry and talk to yourself about them.[2]

Stop often and pray about what you are discovering and feeling. Be frank with God about the disappointing items on your list and about the anger and hatred you feel because of them. Let Him know you are doing this exercise to rid yourself of these feelings, not to foster them.

Much of the exercise's benefit will be gained from compiling the list, which is not to be shown to anyone, especially to your parents. In the next step, Bloomfield describes a safe way to talk about these hurts.

Visualize Your Parent

Alone, in a private place where you won't be disturbed, use your imagination to tell your parents about your bitter experiences with them. With your eyes closed, visualize yourself with one of your parents. Say, "Out of the love that I have for you, and out of the love that I know underneath it all you have for me, there are some things I need to clean up with you." Then, for a half-hour or so, proceed to talk about your list. No need to talk about all the items; in fact, you may end up spending most of the time on one episode or item.

Take time to defend yourself. Tell them how they hurt you; say the things you should have said when you were a child but couldn't because you were defenseless and immature.[3]

Write a Letter

Another exercise gets at your feelings by writing them down in the form of a letter. The letter lists your grievances and shares your feelings just as the first two exercises suggest. Be careful how you handle the strong feelings that result from this exercise. You may want to pound a pillow or even scream; it's important to let go of your feelings, but don't try to generate more. Remember to keep on voicing your feelings to God. Choose someone you can be open and honest with to join you in prayer. Bloomfield suggests you end this exercise on a positive note: "Picture yourself with your parent in a place you would enjoy (such as a park, a beach or perhaps your own home)." Then, picture God's love like a warm light flooding over you.

ANALYZE YOUR ANIMOSITY

You'll need some quiet time to follow this next suggestion:

Analyze and dismiss the need for your resentment. As you read these pages, stop and reflect on your situation. If you completed any of the above exercises, you may already feel liberated from some harsh feelings. You may even feel warmth in your heart previously blocked out. But you may even feel more resentful since you have uncovered more things to be resentful about. Be patient. While I hope you get so much relief you'll feel like a miracle has taken place, I hope you'll realize this is not always the case. People have taken years to lose their hard feelings.

After sorting out why you have bitterness, you can now analyze why you hang onto it. No doubt we are bitter because we choose to be; resentment benefits us in some way and we cling to it like a child does to a security blanket. If we can find out what we get out of it, we may be better able to let go of it. We may find ourselves shrugging our shoulders and saying, "Who needs it anyway?" Test whether or not you have reasons for nursing your resentment by asking yourself the following questions.

1. Am I bitter toward my parents to help my own self-respect? To rise above my parents? Do I feel that I am

better than they are?

Perhaps you are one adult child whose road to self-respect meant putting as much distance as possible between yourself and your parents. Your anger is a wall that puts them on the "other side of the tracks" where they belong. It's not really necessary to reject your parents to feel better about yourself.

2. Am I bitter toward my parents because it helps me feel less guilty about my faults and mistakes? Have I really not taken responsibility for my own behavior?

It makes sense to be angry if your parents have handed you a plateful of personal problems to deal with in adulthood. But resentment isn't justified if it's a way of escaping your own guilt and problems.

3. Am I bitter toward my parents because I'm so down on myself?

4. Am I bitter toward my parents because I don't want to condone what they do? Do I stay angry with them because I don't want to accept them for what they are?

Since Jesus taught us to love sinners, we need not fear that doing so signals we approve of what they do.

5. Am I bitter toward my parents because I want them to change? Am I afraid if I love them as they are, they will stay as they are?

Sometimes we use anger to force other people to change. This is not a good substitute for telling our parents how we feel about their behavior and leaving it with them. Despite the fact that anger is often used in this way, we've got to believe Scripture which says plainly, "Man's anger does not bring about the righteous life that God desires" (James 1:20).

6. Am I bitter toward my parents to punish them for what they have done to me?

Sometimes we withhold things: We keep them from visiting the grandkids, or we constantly pick fights or argue about things. In a variety of ways we let them know we are mad, which is wrong whether our parents have repented or not. "Do not repay anyone evil for evil," wrote the apostle Paul (Romans 12:17). Getting even should not be the Christian's style.

7. Am I bitter toward my parents because I want God or others to punish them for what they did to me? Craving justice, deep down inside you, you may want your parent to receive his or her just desserts. Get in touch with this and deal with it. Scripture explains how.

First, Scripture makes it clear that if we decide not to retaliate, it doesn't mean that the unrepentant offender goes off scot-free. Loving our enemies doesn't make them innocent. The apostle Paul writes: "Do not take revenge, my friends, but leave room for God's wrath, for it is written: `It is mine to avenge; I will repay,' says the Lord. On the contrary, `If your enemy is hungry, feed him; if he is thirsty, give him something to drink. In doing this, you will heap burning coals on his head.' Do not be overcome by evil, but overcome evil with good" (Romans 12:19-21).

The apostle Paul comforted persecuted Christians with the promise that the persecutors would get their due: "God is just: He will pay back trouble to those who trouble you and give relief to you who are troubled, and to us as well. This will happen when the Lord Jesus is revealed from heaven in blazing fire with his powerful angels. He will punish those who do not know God and do not obey the gospel of our Lord Jesus. They will be punished with everlasting destruction and shut out from the presence of the Lord and from the majesty of his power on the day he comes" (2 Thessalonians 1:6-10). If we are holding on to resentment for justice's sake, we don't have to, because God will set things right. We can let go of our bitterness without letting unrepentant parents off the hook.

If you want to rid yourself of a burning desire for vengeance, the Bible doesn't simply tell you to drop it. It tells you to drop it on God. Let Him handle it, and in the process, cast yourself on Him. This, says the apostle Peter, is how to handle suffering. "It is commendable if a man bears up under the pain of unjust suffering because he is conscious of God. . . . To this you were called, because Christ suffered for you, leaving you an example, that you should follow in his steps. . . . When they hurled their insults at him, he did not retaliate; when he suffered, he made no threats. Instead, he entrusted himself to him who judges justly" (1 Peter 2:19-23).

Jesus indicated that we might even be kinder to our enemies than this: "Love your enemies and pray for those who persecute you, that you may be sons of your Father in heaven. He causes his sun to rise on the evil and the good" (Matthew 5:44). Stephen, the first Christian martyr, did this. As he was dying he cried out, "Lord, do not hold this sin against them" (Acts 7:60).

If you are unable to pray such a prayer for the one who victimized you, don't dismay. Examples of those who prayed for judgment show us that we need not always be compelled to pray like Stephen. Regularly manhandled by his persecutors, the apostle Paul shared how he felt about one of them: "Alexander the metalworker did me a great deal of harm. The Lord will repay him for what he has done" (2 Timothy 4:14). In the future, those who are murdered in the time of earth's tribulation impatiently cry out, "How long, Sovereign Lord, holy and true, until you judge the inhabitants of the earth and avenge our blood?" (Revelation 6:10).

Since God will settle our accounts in eternity, we don't
have to harbor bitter feelings now. Tell God how you feel
and let the bitterness go. Release it by talking with a
counselor or a support group. When we air bitter
thoughts, we are not merely griping and complaining. We
are talking of our wounds to people who accept and
understand us and who assure us that we have been
wronged. Their responses validate what we feel: "You are
right; you were wronged."   "Yes, you have been
harmed"; "Certainly, that was terrible"; "The same thing
happened to me"; "Yes, I feel the same way." These
words help adult children realize they aren't crazy, they
haven't made up things, they aren't strange for feeling so
much anger at their parents.

Matt tells what the support group meant to him:

*I was afraid that I would talk too much, or that the others
would not want to hear me, or that perhaps I had no
dysfunctional family background at all. Once I started to
talk, though, the feelings of relief started to flow. The
people I was with listened intently, and I felt that at last I
could understand better why I am the way I am. Why do
I always feel different? I now knew that it was okay to be
different. To have come from an alcoholic home was not
my fault. Somewhere deep down inside, I had been hiding
a false guilt. Now I not only had to deal with guilt, but
also the inevitable feelings of anger toward my family for
their dysfunctional behavior toward me.*

*I still have many feelings of anger toward Dad, but many
of those feelings are being healed now as I continue to
discuss them with my group and my counselor. The
anger and bitterness is still there, but it is being replaced
by feelings of peace as I begin to understand more about
what happened.*

Though Matt's bad feelings toward his dad are
dwindling, his relationship with him is still bad. After he

read the first chapter of this book in manuscript form, he was quite disturbed. What troubled him was the story of how I tried to build a bridge to my father. He wrote on the manuscript: "This really bothers me. My dad is living with a girl who is my age (Matt is 25, his dad is 60) and bitterly fighting my mother over her property. He has also threatened to kill her." Matt had dealt with his father like businessmen do with a bad investment: He wrote him off. He was jolted by my suggestion that he could associate with such a father, let alone benefit from doing so. "So I've forgiven my parents; do I now have to befriend them?"

Sometimes we see forgiveness as a way of separating. We want the rancor out of our system so we can get the person out of our lives. But usually there is more unfinished business to settle with our parents. Fay is a good example of how difficult it is to reconcile yourself to some parents.

I have tried to build a better relationship with my father. All my life I have been defending myself from his harshness and criticisms. It would be so good to clear the air between us. But when I go home to see him, he hardly acknowledges I'm there. Not only doesn't he greet me, but if he is doing something like painting a wall, he just keeps on doing it, never even stopping to look at me.

She hungers for his love and acceptance; she asks for bread and he gives her a stone. Her attempts to discard her bitterness by making things right with him end up creating more.

It's tough to reach out to parents who won't reach back. It's even tougher when they fight back or keep on with their offending ways. This is the case for so many adult children, who continue to face their parent's harsh treatment and alcoholic behavior. Even when a parent is reaching out, relating isn't simple since neither of you fully knew what a normal parent-child relationship was and now aren't sure what a normal parent-adult child relationship should be. Let's now look at the superb guidelines people are discovering to help us build a healthy relationship with our parents, even without their help.

Out of the Nest

It takes a big word like *differentiation* to label the task of making a healthy break from your parents after you've grown up. Most of your unfinished business with them is left over from getting safely out of your parent's nest. In nature as well as society, it can sometimes be a tricky process. The female eagle looks after her eaglet with great care, feeding it regularly until it is strong enough to fend for itself. The big problem the mother faces as the eaglet grows up is that of knowing when the young bird can take care of itself. If she allows it to leave the eyrie before it can make a kill or defend itself, it will perish, either from starvation or from attack by another predator. If she waits too long, the time for the eaglet to learn how to make a kill will have passed. So the process of handing over responsibility to the young bird and of teaching it to survive in the world is a delicate one.

Freedom's Three Forms

In our society, this flight from the nest, differentiation, is complex. Grown kids must attain freedom in three ways: financially, functionally, and emotionally. It involves making enough money to care for yourself without your parent's help. It means being able to make decisions and solve problems without always asking Mom and Dad. You can ask for advice, but you don't burden them with your problems—or blame them for your mistakes.

The emotional tie is more difficult to sever. There are people who live two thousand miles from home and make a six-digit salary who are disastrously shackled to their parents. Most likely they are from a dysfunctional home.[4]

Emotional differentiation means that you feel somewhat free to be yourself. Ideally, you prayerfully choose a path based on your gifts, inclinations, and opportunities. You make your own decisions about your vocation, life-style, values, etc. In the process you consider carefully your parent's advice, and in the end you may be a lot like them, but you have chosen for yourself.

Stuck in the Nest

Failure to differentiate can take one of two forms. First, you may follow your parent's wishes or choose their ways without careful thought and freedom. You're more of a xerox copy than an original. A Christian girl I know shocked the people in her church by leaving her husband and having an affair. When we talked with her she said it was because she never carved out her own life. She became a Christian to please her parents and married one for the same reason. Because she conformed too much earlier, she chose to rebel later. Thankfully, she changed her mind and decided she would remain loyal to her marriage partner.

If you don't become your own person you may end up adopting your parents' negative traits. "I began to turn to the bottle for inner peace just like my dad had done," and "I resorted to yelling and screaming just like Mom," are statements of undifferentiated adult children.

Rebellion against parents is another form of being undifferentiated. It also keeps you under their spell. To show you what I mean, let's talk in color. Color your family blue. To be properly differentiated you'll probably become purple. You'll obviously be like your parents in many ways, but because you have been properly, systematically free to choose your own ways, you have become somewhat different from your parents. If you grow up entirely blue, you are probably not properly differentiated since all of us are different in some ways. If you rebel it is because you rejected your parents and what they stand for. Then you may choose to be red—anything that doesn't resemble blue. You experiment with casual sex because your parents don't think it's moral. You take drugs because they're against it. You may think you have become your own person, but you have actually done the same thing as a person who conforms. Both are a matter of being unduly influenced. Perhaps God meant for you to be green, but you have chosen red—all because of your parents.

Being out of the nest allows you to face your parents in an adult way. That translates into your allowing them to be themselves and their allowing you to be yourself. It means you handle your responsibilities and they handle theirs.

It doesn't take much imagination to see how hard it might be to extract oneself from a dysfunctional family. Because these families are chained together around a dominant problem, there is a tendency to hang on to one another or escape from one another in unhealthy ways. Lack of detachment shows up in our group every time we meet: "My dad called me last night and complained how Mom is such a problem to him. Yet he's the alcoholic. I feel so depressed that I can hardly keep up with my classes." Or it appears as a subtle loneliness: "I miss my dad even though I hate him." Often it comes in the form of intense anxiety: "I worry all the time about whether or not my father will hurt my mother."

CHANGING THE RELATIONSHIP
WITHOUT BREAKING IT

Letting go of resentment toward parents is no problem for some adults; letting go of their parents is. Overinvolvement in a parent's problem is one symptom of this. When an adult child tells me she is failing courses because she is so wrapped up in her parents' impending divorce, then she is enmeshed in the family system.

Another symptom is being too concerned about what they think. "I was depressed all last week thinking about going home this summer to live with my parents." That from a twenty-nine-year-old man who felt obligated to go back home to an alcoholic family. "I'm going home this summer; my parents want me to stay in our house, but I want to get my own apartment. When things get bad at home, I need a place to run to to get my head together. But I'll probably stay with them. I hate to hurt their feelings. I don't know what I would tell them."

Some parents don't want to push their kids out of the nest. They depend too much on their children and make their children too dependent on them. We have already shown how co-dependency is the hallmark of a dysfunctional home. These families fail to draw normal boundaries around each other. Instead they draw a line around the whole family and cinch it in. Individual interests, goals, and identities are somewhat denied to keep the system functioning around the dominant problem, be it anger, abuse, alcoholism, work, or legalistic religious practice. Everyone conforms to the way of life that is woven around the central addiction.

Strong emotional ties may continue to make them feel responsible for the welfare of their parents and siblings long into adulthood. This unhealthy attachment can interfere with their own marriages, disrupt their personal goals, and wreak havoc on their emotions. Sometimes, they are so abnormally engulfed by their families that they even resent others suggesting they are too concerned.

Not long ago a seminary student came to ask me how she could help her mother deal with her alcoholic father and her rebellious brother. She was considering dropping out of school to go home to put things right. She was losing sleep over her mother's plight and deeply distressed by the regular phone calls from her. When I suggested that her family might be too dependent on her, she took a very defensive attitude. "Should I not love them?" she challenged. Certainly she should. But how? Love takes many forms. Christian love can be summed up in a phrase: "Doing what is best for the other's highest good." Being a co-dependent falls short of that definition.

Drawing New Boundaries

The co-dependent's problem is one of boundaries. To be separate from your parents, you must develop your own identity apart from them. You do not continue to feel about yourself the way you feel about them. You must not feel they have to get their act together before you can feel right about yourself. When you feel this way, you become obsessed with solving someone else's problem because it has become your problem. Your nervous system is plugged into that person's actions. He stubs his toe and you say ouch. Dad drinks and you feel guilty. Mom and Dad fight and you get depressed. Often, your pain is greater than theirs. Co-dependents permit themselves to become victims of someone else's problems. These questions will help you decide if your emotional ties to your family are too tight:

1. Do you think you know what is best for your parents?

2. Do you need your parents' approval?

3. When your parents hurt do you seem to feel it more than they do?

4. If members of your family have a bad day, do you react?

5. Do you feel you must solve your parent's problems?

6. Do you respond more to your family's interests than develop your own?

7. Do you limit your involvement with others because of your family?

8. Do you think you can convince members of your family to like themselves?

9. Do you consider carefully what you say to your parents in order to get the right reaction from them?

10. Do you feel guilty when you take care of yourself?

If you said yes to three or four of these, you may be more dependent than is good for you or your parents. Though your compassion is commendable, you may not be loving for the right reasons. You'll get nothing but frustration from trying to solve someone else's problems in order to feel better about yourself.

Is it right to meet someone else's need simply because of a need to be needed? Co-dependency is known to do weird things to people. Wives of alcoholics seem to invest their whole being into getting their husbands to stop drinking. But when their husbands go on the wagon, they get depressed, unconsciously wishing the husband would go back to the bottle. This is because they have built their lives around solving a problem; once the problem is solved, they have little or nothing to live for.

This leads to the major reason we should avoid being needlessly attached to our parents: It does them no good.

We may think we are helping them when all the while we are hindering them. They depend on us to solve their problem instead of solving it for themselves, and as long as we are willing to take their problem, they won't own it themselves. As long as we protect them from the consequences, they won't feel the results of their wrongdoing. Kids, as well as anyone else, cannot learn to be responsible as long as there is someone who constantly says, "Here, let me do it for you."

Certainly the Bible says, "Carry each other's burdens, and in this way you will fulfill the law of Christ" (Galatians 6:2). Yet a few sentences later it warns, "Each one shall bear his own load" (Galatians 6:5, NASB). The different Greek words used for *burden* and *load* explain the difference. Burdens are like rocks too heavy for one person to handle; but a load is like a backpack, representing what we are personally responsible for carrying. When we take someone else's assigned backpack, we rob him of the opportunity to solve his own problems and develop inner strength. Love means doing what's best for someone; feeling and doing for people what they should be feeling and doing for themselves is not in their best interests. While it permits you to have good feelings, it allows them to continue bad habits.

Detach

To get out of this co-dependency trap, you have to become detached. You must signal to them that you will no longer bear their problem. This is not the same as abandoning them or denouncing them. You have probably tried that already. Usually co-dependence fluctuates from being overly kind to being overly angry. One day we protect, help, forgive, utter kind soothing words of comfort. "It's okay; I'm here; I'll take care of you." Then we get disgusted and we threaten, blame, and attack. "This is the last time I'll help you; don't bother me with your problems." Detachment means you must first emotionally cut the tie between their problems and your welfare. You must surrender the enormous need you have for them to be straightened out.

You must change your thinking: You must come to believe that your life doesn't depend on solving your parents' problems. You must get rid of the notion that they have to be okay before you feel okay. Sure, you'll still care; you'll still try to help in the right way. But you cut the tie; their problem is their problem, not yours. You will no longer tie your welfare to the outcome of their lives. Once that is done, you will communicate that to them. Actually, you won't even have to tell them; they will see it in your attitude and your actions.

If your parents are very dependent on you, they will accuse you of being unconcerned and unloving. They may even suggest that you are betraying them. You will have to remember that they are threatened when you refuse to show the same kind of intense care, because they will have to care for themselves. If you aren't worried anymore, they will have to worry. You'll need to say things that support them but don't do it for them: "I know you can handle it," instead of, "When I get home I'll take care of it." "I know you'll find a way out," instead of, "I'll think about it and call you back with some advice." "I feel great about what's happening in my life; sorry you are having such difficulty," instead of "I really feel crushed that this is going on with you." Once you really get emotionally detached it will show.

You must also get detached in a practical way. This entails refusing to do for them what they should do for themselves. A biblical proverb makes it very clear that we must allow people to face the consequences of their own mistakes. "A hot-tempered man must pay the penalty; if you rescue him, you will have to do it again" (Proverbs 19:19). The offender has to hit bottom to be jolted into admitting he or she has a problem.

Not only will you have to stop bailing out the parent with the problem, but you will have to stop helping the other parent bail him or her out.

Co-dependents and enablers must sometimes hit bottom themselves before they admit what they are doing. They are so entrenched in their rescue operations that it takes a bout with a bleeding ulcer or severe depression to shake them awake. Even after they decide to stop their enabling, it isn't always easy to do so. One of the men in our group sent money regularly to his mother, who was always financially in trouble because of her drinking. During several trips home a year he put in a supply of wood to heat her house because the money to pay for her gas bill was squandered on alcohol. Shutting down his support of her habit took a lot of courage.

This is why many experts claim most co-dependents can't unchain themselves without help from others. A counselor or support group helps them withstand the mixture of guilt, fear, and pity that pressures them to take back the problem. They can help you distinguish between an abnormal sense of responsibility and a sensible concern.

Healthy Concern, Not Worried Sick

Love is costly; we cannot love someone who hurts without hurting. But concern is different from the co-dependent's obsessive anxiety. Scripture charges, "Do not be anxious about anything, but in everything, by prayer and petition, with thanksgiving, present your requests to God" (Philippians 4:6). Replace any obsessive anxious attempts to rescue or change your family with intelligent actions. There will be things you can do to assist them in facing their problem without solving it for them.

Along with praying for them, you can try to teach them about dysfunctional families. Read about your family's particular problem. Talk about the problem with any family member who will listen to you. Break the dysfunctional rule of not talking . . . discuss the cover-up. Change the way you act in the family, but be prepared to be attacked. The first member of a dysfunctional family to see through the deception is usually in for it. The system's strong denial is tough to break through.

You may take steps to protect brothers and sisters. You can do for them what you wish others would have done for you. If they are young children, talk to them about their feelings and find out how they are handling the abuse or the alcoholism. In the case of abuse, you may have to consult a pastor or counselor who can look into the matter and report it to a social worker who can take professional action. You must resist the temptation to continue to protect the offender; you must do something for those he or she is hurting.

Planned Intervention

Often, all you can do is go on with your life while you prayerfully, patiently wait for your parents to get so fed up with the situation that they are ready to do something about it. Sometimes they can be spared from the worst consequences by a properly conducted "intervention." Social workers or personnel in various treatment centers will help you decide whether or not your family would be ready for such a procedure. The alcoholic, for example, may have already gotten some harsh signals that life is out of control: a ticket for drunk driving, constant arguments at home, a couple of blackouts. The next step is bad health, a jail sentence, and loss of job. An intervention might save him from the final stages of his destructive plunge.

It is a carefully planned confrontation. Members of the family join an expert to point out kindly, not harshly, the evidence of the problem. Usually, a person who has recovered from the same problem is there to sympathize with the person's struggle. Family members don't accuse, but explain how badly they feel and how they have been hurt by the parent's actions. At the slightest glimmer of readiness, the person is persuaded to immediately check into a treatment center.

Adult to Adult

By no means should the adult child's relationship with the parents be centered around the problem. If initial efforts to get the family to face the problem fail, you should then accept life with the problem. You don't ignore it, but you don't feel responsible for making it go away; and you do nothing to support the family in denying or perpetuating it.

The dysfunctional family will try to keep you in the child-parent relationship. "I hate to go home because when I do my mom treats me like I am nine years old. The problem is that I respond to her like I am nine." Home brings out the child in you, but you can't wait until Mom stops treating you like a nine-year-old before you grow up; you have to stop responding like one. The best thing you can do for yourself and your parents is try to establish an adult-to-adult relationship with them.

Analyze your family; if there was an immature behavior, you probably learned an immature response. If you looked at a dysfunctional family as being sick, as many experts do, you have to realize you are sick too. You must not expect to heal the family before you heal yourself. The beauty of this approach is that you need not necessarily avoid your family to grow as a person. The challenge is to learn to be healthy in the midst of their illness. Some adult children think it's almost impossible to do so. One middle-aged woman in our group said she would be terrified to defend herself against her mother's criticisms. "When she says you're stupid, why not tell her how stupid it is to call someone stupid?" we asked. She was horrified at the thought.

One member of our group told of his struggle to change:

> *I went home for a visit and it was the usual pattern. My father and I got into a big argument. I stood up to him and defended myself. My dad packed a suitcase and left. I knew that he would be back later in the evening. But there was one difference this time; my mother told me later that he didn't mean the things he said, because he had been drinking. I was amazed to realize that I had been arguing violently all these years with him without really knowing that the problem was alcoholism. Now I can face the situation differently. I am now beginning to see that he is picking on me, not because of my shortcomings but because of his addiction. I can begin to change my childlike reactions to him.*

In an adult-to-adult relationship, each person permits the other to be himself. The typical dysfunctional family will not allow this. Parents give an immature response and the young adult reacts with a childish gesture. "My father objected severely to my going to seminary. I just left and never went back home again for six years," reported one man. "Now, I have gone back home; I just ignore my dad's criticisms and realize that I must build my own life. He's even begun to back off his criticisms of me now that I am facing him like an adult."

Another in our group reported good progress: "My mother has made me so angry. She calls almost every morning at 8:00 A.M. She does this on Saturday despite the fact that she knows I want to sleep in. Now, instead of just getting upset, I have told her not to call Saturday morning. I'm not sure she will listen to me, but it has made me feel better to react with assertion instead of anger."

It may take time to learn mature interpersonal skills. Further chapters will offer some practical guidelines, and as you use these skills in your phone calls, letters, and visits with your parents, the effects will be dramatic. Focusing on them instead of yourself or the problems between you is a way of showing Christlike love and building a more positive relationship. Study their backgrounds. Ask them about their childhoods and past experiences. Put questions to friends and relatives that will help you know your parents better. As you learn about their history, you will be composing your own, which, despite the family problems, will help you know better who you are.

You may find good things in the past that help balance some of the bad. You'll no doubt uncover some roots of your family problems. It seems strange to me now that I never once asked my father about his father and how they got along. An aged aunt, my dad's sister, provided just a little peek into their childhood home when she said, "We never shared our feelings with one another." After hearing that, my own relationship to my father was less of a mystery. Too bad the insight came in the hospital hallway outside the room where my father lay dying. Many questions remain. Did their not talking about feelings mean they lacked intimacy? Were they close in other ways? Were they acting like the typical German family of their day, or were there alcoholics in their background?

Sharing Christ

When your parent/adult child relationship is improved, you are in a better position to share Christ with non-Christian parents. But adult children must avoid becoming obsessed with leading their parents to Christ, just as they were in changing them in other ways. We must offer them the same freedom to choose their values, faith, and lifestyle as we expect from them. Otherwise, we continue in our co-dependency. Instead of sharing Christ, we end up arguing about religion, and our parents feel compelled to agree with us instead of invited to make their own decision.

To avoid this, we will have to break the bonds of co-dependency and keep reminding ourselves that we are not held accountable for our parents' salvation. We will wait upon the Holy Spirit for the best time to share Christ with them. Above all, we must struggle to discern when our obligation ends and our parents' begins, giving us liberty from an agonizing burden and giving them freedom to decide for themselves.

Avoid thinking that you can't have any closeness until they come to Christ. Not only a common faith, but love can be the basis of a spirit of kinship. The gifted evangelist, the apostle Paul, instructed: "If it is possible, as far as it depends on you, live at peace with everyone" (Romans 12:18).

Become Friends

In his men's seminar, David Simmons, a former cornerback for the Dallas Cowboys, tells about his childhood home. His father, a military man, was extremely demanding, rarely saying a kind word, always pushing him with harsh criticism to do better. The father had decided that he would never permit his son to feel any satisfaction from his accomplishments, reminding him there were always new goals ahead. When Dave was a little boy, his dad gave him a bicycle, unassembled, with the command that he put it together. After Dave struggled to the point of tears with the difficult instructions and many parts, his father said, "I knew you couldn't do it." Then he assembled it for him.

When Dave played football in high school, his father was unrelenting in his criticisms. In the backyard of his home, after every game, his dad would go over every play and point out Dave's errors. "Most boys got butterflies in the stomach before the game; I got them afterwards. Facing my father was more stressful than facing any opposing team." By the time he entered college, Dave hated his father and his harsh discipline. He chose to play football at the University of Georgia because its campus was further from home than any school that offered him a scholarship.

After college, he became the second round draft pick of the St. Louis Cardinal's professional football club. Joe Namath (who later signed with the New York Jets), was the club's first round pick that year. "Excited, I telephoned my father to tell him the good news. He said 'How does it feel to be second?' "

Despite the hateful feelings he had for his father, Dave began to build a bridge to his dad. Christ had come into his life during college years, and it was God's love that made him turn to his father. During visits home he stimulated conversation with him and listened with interest to what his father had to say. He learned for the first time what his grandfather had been like—a tough lumberjack known for his quick temper. Once he destroyed a pickup truck with a sledgehammer because it wouldn't start, and he often beat his son. This new awareness affected Dave dramatically. "Knowing about my father's upbringing not only made me more sympathetic for him, but it helped me see that, under the circumstances, he might have done much worse. By the time he died, I can honestly say we were friends."

LIVE WITHOUT THE BLESSING

Not all parent/adult child relationships will end as this one did. Sometimes we have to be brutally frank with ourselves and acknowledge that we may never get the approval we seek, the love we yearn for. Our parents may be too indifferent or too wrapped up in their own struggles. This we must finally come to accept.

After all, it is possible to live without your parent's blessing. We ourselves need not be unhealthy because our relationships to our parents were. We need not be handicapped or feel incomplete or imperfect. Personal histories show us that other adults can supply for us what we missed from our parents. Countless children grow up without their natural parents or with neglectful, abusive ones without being scarred. Adult children can overcome the loss of good parenting. Usually, there is a struggle involved, and you may have to grieve extensively. Sometimes adult children refrain from grieving by taking their loss of a happier childhood too lightly. "No big deal," they say to themselves, all the while ignoring the depression and anger typical of grief. In the next chapter, we'll look at how we can more properly handle our grief.

Accepting the losses of your past life involves getting on with your present life. So you can't make much of the past; you *can* make much of the present. We do this by not being compelled to repeat it. We refuse to tell ourselves things like, "My dad was a drunk; what do you expect of me?" We also do it by not trying to "make up" for the past. We must repair damages—emotions and behaviors that hurt us and others, but we have to avoid

174 Part Two: Resolving the Past

putting the past, present, and future in columns in an attempt to balance them out. "Because of my shame for my past, I'll prove to the world I'm worthwhile." "Because I failed to stop my dad from drinking, I'll cure as many alcoholics as I can or die trying."

Being someone who is worthwhile is commendable; helping treat alcoholics is great; but we must not do these things to prove ourselves or offset our supposed failures. A person may counsel drunks or may be a drunk because he is the injured child of an alcoholic. Either scenario will keep him enslaved to his past. Instead, we must write off our losses and get on with today.

Notes

1. Harold Bloomfield, *Making Peace with Your Parents* (New York: Ballentine Books, 1983), p. 30.

2. Ibid., pp. 33, 34.

3. Ibid., p. 32.

4. Timmen L. Cermak and Stephanie Brown, "Interactional Group Therapy with the Adult Children of Alcoholics," *International Journal of Group Psychotherapy* 32 (July 1982): 377.

RESOLVE

Though we know many of our emotional problems are due to our past, we will seek to deal with them in the present.

8

Coping with Emotional Problems

I f you talk long with adult children about themselves, the subject of emotions will come up. "My problem is anxiety," one will say. Another will explain that depression troubles him most.

Nothing baffles us like our emotions, and so much of the adult child's struggle is emotional. Changing how we think is much simpler than changing how we feel. If we lack a definition of happiness, we can find it in the dictionary. But if we lack happiness, we aren't sure where to look or what to do. Problems with guilt, fear, depression, grief, shame, and anxiety demand solutions for many adult children, for our feelings affect the way we think about ourselves and our ability to be intimate with others.

THINKING RIGHT ABOUT FEELING WRONG

How we look at our emotional troubles is crucial. Sometimes they are so out of whack we think of them as wounded. It's popular to talk of the *healing* of *damaged* feelings. It might also be harmful. There are only a few times when the Bible uses the terms *sickness* and *healing* to refer to something other than a physical ailment. In these cases the words are used metaphorically, not literally, to talk of spiritual struggles, not emotional ones (Hebrews 12:13; 1 Peter 2:24; Matthew 13:15; Isaiah 6:10). It is by no means clear that James refers to emotional healing when he urges us to pray for one another that we may be "healed," since the context strongly suggests physical healing.

In the New Testament, people with emotional struggles were often pictured as demon possessed, not sick. Without being dogmatic about such a complex issue, I would like to suggest how picturing our emotions as sick or damaged might hinder how we properly handle them. I am not denying that people can be emotionally or mentally sick, nor am I excluding the possibility that physical disease, illness, or problems are behind emotional problems, as when a shortage of chemicals in the brain causes depression.

What concerns me is how describing emotions as being sick, injured, or wounded may divert our attention from the real problem. When we think of something as sick or damaged, we think of it as not working properly. A mechanic working on a stalled Ford or a surgeon performing an operation has to first discover what's wrong in order to repair it. Apply this same strategy to feelings like anger, depression, or anxiety and you raise a difficult question: What's damaged about them? It's almost impossible to locate the injured part of a feeling.

If a man is depressed, is it because his "happiness" is wounded? If a woman has a "bad temper," exactly what is wrong with her anger mechanism? I know men who get into first class screaming, yelling rages almost daily.

Yet I can see nothing wrong with their anger: It works far better than most people's.

The problem lies elsewhere, and that is what we can easily overlook whenever we think our emotions are sick. It turns them into mysteriously injured parts of us which we don't know how to fix because we can't quite describe what's wrong. This sometimes keeps people from dealing with them at all.

We don't blame someone for feeling bad if they are genuinely sick; sickness is socially acceptable. So using the terms *damaged* or *sick* becomes an easy excuse for failing to face our problems.

How Do You Fix Fear?

Even if we try to repair our damaged emotions, we are going to be hard pressed to know how to fix them. What do you do for a damaged temper or a wounded fear or sick guilt? Helplessness turns to hopelessness, and the adult child easily falls into the victim mode, complaining, "My parents damaged my temper and I can do nothing about it."

If the "sick person" does do something about it, he or she looks for some special remedy, like alcohol, drugs, or medicine. Or else the mysterious and wounded emotion calls for a mysterious and spiritual treatment. Pray a certain prayer, do a special ritual, and the damage is healed.

I strongly advocate praying for God's supernatural grace to work in our lives. And I advocate the use of medicines to treat certain emotional problems. But the bulk of our emotional hangups are not as baffling as they seem, and they don't require some cure. They require change—in our thinking and in our behavior. Thankfully, there are practical measures we can take to solve our emotional problems, even those that stem from severe parental abuse, neglect, or incest.

Change the Picture, Change the Approach

For starters, we have to stop saying things like, "I have a damaged temper," and start saying things like, "I get angry a lot." This changes the picture we have of our feelings from something wrong with us to some wrong we do. It means that we own our feelings instead of saying someone has crippled us beyond repair. We find solutions when we turn from asking what we can do for damaged anger to what we can do to keep from getting angry.

Let's look at another example. A woman may picture herself as sexually wounded. If she is married and her lack of sexual desire for her husband becomes a problem, notice how it might help to change her statement from "I am sexually wounded" to "I am afraid of men." Then she can ask herself, "What can I do to be less afraid of my husband," rather than, "What will heal my injured sexuality?"

If her problem was caused by incest, her father didn't damage her sexuality. Doing something forbidden to her aroused feelings of fear and disgust. Her capacity for fear and disgust were not hurt at all; in fact, they were functioning quite normally. Her problem now is that they are still functioning when they shouldn't—when she is about to have sex with her husband.

To see what's happening to her, picture her feelings of fear and disgust as guardian lions. Whenever she gets near a sexual situation, they spring to their feet, growling and roaring their protest, shutting off her sexual feelings, just as they did with her dad. Her sexual feelings are not damaged; they are hindered. Her feelings of fear and disgust are working quite well and don't need fixing; they need retraining.

There are things she can do to make her feelings recognize the difference between atrocious, ugly sex with a father and acceptable, lovely sex with a husband. It's possible that coming to Christ as Savior and seeing that God created her as a woman and sex as a gift will radically change her attitude and still the lions. A particular experience or something an authority says or verses of Scripture might change her mind. It's also possible it may take her and her husband years of patient effort to slowly retrain her feelings so that she can respond positively to his touch.

According to some psychologists, most of our emotional problems are defensive responses rooted in our past. A woman who angrily attacks people may have started doing that with a father who abusively attacked her. A man who feels depressed most of the time may be feeling the sadness he felt when he witnessed daily fights between his mother and father. He could have reacted in other ways: angry rebellion (stomping out of the house and disobeying them by taking drugs) or by covering up with humor (becoming the family clown, trying to laugh off the hurts of life). In other words, our emotions are learned.

When they are a problem to us it is because: 1) We have mistaken a reason for feeling an emotion (like feeling guilty when your dad divorced your mother or you couldn't stop your mother from drinking); 2) We no longer have a reason to feel a certain emotion but we continue to feel it (like fearing impending doom because you used to be afraid terrible things would happen when your father got angry with you). We don't just pray such emotions away or make them vanish with forty Scripture verses. Prayer and memorizing Scripture will be strategic, along with God's grace. But the process of dealing with our emotions lies less in God's supernatural power to heal them than it does in His giving us supernatural power, love, and patience to retrain them.

In this chapter, I'll suggest a two-pronged approach to this retraining process. I will suggest ways to confront our emotions by encountering our pasts. Thankfully, doing so may actually shrink our depression, fear, and anxiety by reducing their power in our lives. I will also discuss tactics for dealing with emotions in the present, because looking backward is not treatment enough.

GOING BACK FOR THE FUTURE

Identify Past Feelings

Because the past is still present in your mind, there are ways to make some profitable visits to it. Before I explain what I mean, let me tell you about one of my visits. One day I was exploring my own emotional connection with my past by completing an exercise recommended for adult children.[1] It guided me on an imaginary visit to my childhood home, using a comfortable chair to shuttle me back in time.

Since my memories were mostly happy ones, I had nothing to fear. I "flew" back on my Illinois office chair to Pennsylvania, lingering first on the front porch, then making my way through the living room and kitchen, trying to trigger memories of the past. Tears ran down my cheeks as memories evoked a nostalgic mixture of joy and sadness. Yet no new memories surfaced as I searched for them in one room after another.

About ten minutes into my "visit," I realized I was falling short of the assignment's objective. In my imagination I was only visiting home as an adult instead of living there as a child. I then shifted my thinking more than forty years backward in time. I became the little boy in the brown living room chair next to the stair rail looking over at the white enameled piano. My mood changed, suddenly and dramatically: I felt depressed. At once, I recognized the feeling. Though I have never been severely depressed, I do have my share of blue moods. I was in one of them now. Startled, I "returned" to my office to ponder what had happened. It was much later that I made a stunning discovery: My typical depressive feelings were now reduced significantly.

I'm not exactly sure what occurred during that visit, but I've found an explanation that makes sense. My experience can be summed up in some of the steps for confronting annoying emotions. First, discover the "child within" by trying to get an accurate picture of your childhood emotions. Our tendency to deny, distort, and forget makes it imperative to take a closer look at what we were like then.

The depression I felt on my imaginary visit surprised me because I never pictured myself as that unhappy. Further investigation convinced me my typical bouts of depression were present then, making it plausible that the depression I feel today is due in part to the depressed child within me. Perhaps the mere knowledge of this had reduced its power over me. Unconsciously I said to myself, "The cause of that depression is in the past; you don't have to feel that way any longer."

It's liberating to be logical about your emotional responses. If a girl's father abandoned her and she still (wrongly) feels guilty about it, it puts her in a better position to shed herself of false guilt. Once we connect unexplained feelings to our past, we can cut the connection.

As an adult child you need to remind yourself over and over that many of today's feelings were created by childish responses to harsh situations. They were our only defense then, but they aren't appropriate now. Not all troublesome feelings are so easily dealt with; there is another step you will usually need to take.

Relive the Feeling

When I made that mental trip home, I not only recalled the feeling, I reexperienced it. Many experts believe that reliving feelings gets them out of the storage closet of our souls into the open where we can handle them. Be cautious when you do it, because an imaginary visit to childhood could be traumatic. If you expect to uncork sizable pain and emotions, you would do well to have a counselor help you.

Also, be careful not to overdo the re-creation of childhood feelings. In our support groups we observe people with a tendency to retell again and again the horrible things that were done to them in an attempt to get the anger and hurt out of their systems. We have to beware of picturing our emotions like underground oil that needs dredging up until it's all gone. In the process of "getting out all the anger" we may actually be creating more of it, making it seem like the reservoir will never be empty. We remain victims, forever stuck in the past.[2] The major purpose for recalling and reliving our childhood emotions is contained in the next step.

THE ADULT TREATMENT

The big payoff in studying your childhood emotions is that you can do something with them today that you couldn't when you were a child: You can now handle them in an adult way. We can retrain the reactions of our childhood—reactions that helped us take care of ourselves then but aren't appropriate now.

True Admission

First of all, admit how you feel. As children we may have denied certain feelings either because we were ashamed of them or because we couldn't handle them. Made to feel guilty about these feelings, we didn't dare admit, even to ourselves, that we were depressed, unhappy, or angry. Now, we must tell ourselves that it's okay to feel. No longer ashamed of emotions, we should set ourselves free to experience the whole range of human feelings, from sadness to gladness. Adult children tell me that this freedom to feel is one of the most important factors in their recovery.

Psychologist Larry Crabb claims that the Christian community often promotes this deception. Supposed to be new creatures in Christ, people are required to "pretend that they have been transformed."[3] If the Christian's family or church handles uncomfortable feelings by denying them, the person trying to be honest about his feelings will feel like a traitor. A voice inside says, "Of course we are a happy family; what's wrong with you?"

Perhaps there were happy moments, lots of them; but we must not allow the happy moments to blot out the painful ones that need resolution.

Make a Claim

After admitting a feeling, claim it as your own. Victims remain victims until they take charge of their own lives. One expert on stress put it clearly: "We must never claim `My parents make me angry.' No one can make us angry. We must say, `I become angry at my parents.' " He also claims that there are no stressful conditions, only stressed people. Stress is not outside but inside us. Situations don't create stress; we create stress in response to them. Before we can give our anger to God, we must recognize it is ours to give. We must take responsibility for it, something especially difficult for angry people.

Spouse abusers, for example, generally believe that their emotions are basic traits that are given to them over which they can exercise no control.[4] To them emotions are "passions" by which people are "gripped," "seized," or "torn." This is typical of the "storage tank" image of anger. As mistreated children, we denied our anger, pushing it back into the subconscious part of ourselves. Now it is like a thick, menacing fluid stored in an inner tank ready to burst when the pressure gets high enough and someone provokes us. Even if we try to contain it, it will pop out where we least expect it—we'll kick the dog or yell at the kids or turn on a friend.

While this picture of anger may be accurate, we must be careful not to let it mislead us into continuing to blame the past. We must shift from seeing anger as something given to us in the past to something we now do in the present. Dealing with anger starts when we say to ourselves, "I get angry," instead of "I have anger."

Feelings Don't Tame Easily

Christians are responsible for their emotions, according to the New Testament. "Everyone should be quick to listen, slow to speak and slow to become angry," (James 1:19). "Rid yourselves of . . . anger, rage, malice," commands Paul (Colossians 3:8). We died with Christ, potentially rendering powerless the old nature's anger, wrath, malice, evil desires, jealousy, hatred, lust, greed, etc. "Those who belong to Christ Jesus have crucified the sinful nature with its passions and desires" (Galatians 5:24). Raised with Christ we strive, by the Holy Spirit's power, to attain new life (Colossians 3:5-9, Galatians 2:20).

Commands like these should not mislead us into thinking that change is easy. As we mentioned previously, the Christian struggles with a sinful nature, success coming neither automatically nor easily. "The sinful nature desires what is contrary to the Spirit, and the Spirit what is contrary to the sinful nature. They are in conflict with each other, so that you do not do what you want" (Galatians 5:17). Victory over this nature is assured only because Christ's death on the cross stripped sin of its power over us. Although the old nature is potentially powerless, it is made so only as we moment by moment consider ourselves dead to sin and put our trust in the Holy Spirit. Our primary approach to our personal problems is to maintain a close walk with the Lord and do all we can to tackle our problems.

Watch for Negative Patterns

Adult children learned to respond to emotions in ways that hurt them more than helped them. The adult child needs to discover those negative patterns and learn new ones.

A young woman and I were recently discussing her angry disposition. Upset at the slightest annoyance, she was demolishing her marriage. We studied her anger like detectives. At one point I asked her how she felt when her anger subsided. "I slump into depression," she replied. We discovered she also felt depressed before getting angry. While it is possible that her depression was caused by her anger, the reverse may also be true: She gets angry to overcome her depression. Through the years she has learned that being red hot feels better than being blue. To get adrenalin pumping through her system and overcome her depression she finds something to get angry about. Her treatment now focuses on her depression, not her anger. Her task is not just to learn to stop being angry but to start treating her depression in other ways.

Note Your Responses

You would not have been depressed as a child without doing something about it, perhaps withdrawing to your room and reading or enjoying a hobby. Sometimes our reactions were not so wholesome. Once you identify a troubling emotion as part of the adult child within you, you may want to examine how you have responded to that emotion through the years. If it is guilt, ask yourself what you have been doing to deal with it. Are you an overachiever? How have you tried to redeem yourself? Do you criticize others to make yourself feel justified?

Take another emotion: depression. What do you do to cope? One adult child explains:

Excitement has been my ticket out of the emotional pits. Only in my recent self-examination have I been able to see that I have to be going somewhere or doing something to escape feeling blue. I have never been able to understand why I have felt depressed being in my own home, even though being a husband and father has been one of my highest priorities. Now I believe I have the answer. In my youth, when things were bad at home, I felt dejected. To get myself up, I escaped the house; when I was home, I had to be busy doing something. Since discovering this, I have been enjoying a newfound contentment at home, though at times I still feel down. Now I am learning other ways to cope, though I am still sometimes confused about what to do.

There are special ways of looking at and treating some of our most troubling emotions. Let's look at some of them.

ANGER: A GOOD EMOTION THAT'S SOMETIMES BAD

Anger is a human emotion that we need to accept as part of our humanity. Jesus experienced it. The apostle Paul didn't equate anger with sin when he warned, "In your anger do not sin" (Ephesians 4:26). Anger itself is not wrong, but it can lead us to do wrong.

When Anger Is Not Okay

Anger is negative when it is not justified. Cain is a biblical example of a person who was angry without a proper cause. When Abel's offering was accepted, while Cain's was not, Cain became very angry. As far as we can tell from the brief biblical account in Genesis 4, Cain had no basis for being angry with God or his brother.

When interpersonal problems are not dealt with, they eventually create a lot of anger, as Margaret has discovered. Wanting her children to like her, Margaret is afraid to confront them. But when her nice words and gestures don't work, she resents them and ends up going into a rage. She's angry because her children need her discipline, and cause trouble and don't listen. These things she should expect and accept, but because she doesn't, her anger crops up in the wrong places—like when a glass of milk is spilled. If we are unduly angry over other people's mistakes and shortcomings which they can't help, we are wrong.

Another abuse of anger relates to its fruit. Sometimes people do inappropriate things when angry. When carried to the extreme, Cain's anger resulted in murdering his brother. The apostle Paul warns against hatred, slander, and brawling. Apparently, abused children become abusers because they learned to accept inappropriate expressions of anger. Maybe they observed their irate parent slapping a sister on the face because she

knocked over a glass of Kool Aid. As adults, they may justify harsh words or cruel beatings because they were led to believe they deserved such treatment when they were kids.

I know men who scream at their children, their faces contorted by rage, who say the problem in their family is that their wives and children won't accept them as they are. They have become so used to monstrous proportions of anger that they can't recognize it for what it is.

Sometimes adult children learn outrageous forms of anger from fighting as well as watching the parent, as was the case with Kathy.   Her father constantly hurled harsh insults and criticisms at her. To protect herself, she hurled them back. Accustomed to retaliating, she is ever in trouble with her bosses at work where the slightest disapproval or show of anger from them sets her off. What she dreads most is how she will react when her little girl becomes a "terrible two" who challenges her authority.

Anger is also wrong when it is uncontrollable and impulsive. The ill-tempered person in Scripture is the one who is easily angered. "A hot-tempered man stirs up dissension, but a patient man calms a quarrel" (Proverbs 15:18). Being short on temper is a major-league struggle for some adult children. They describe their anger as a caged monster they are never quite sure when they'll turn loose.

Control, a major issue in a troubled home, may be the main reason for excessive and impulsive anger when unpleasant things happen (an unexpected bill) or when caught in uncontrollable circumstances (delayed in heavy traffic) or another person doesn't comply with your wishes (a child refuses to go to bed). In the original language of Proverbs 14:29, being quick-tempered is compared to having a short nose or having shortness of breath. The wise man has a long nose (is patient) while the fool is short of breath (quick tempered). The patient person takes a deep breath as he holds his anger in abeyance. For example, the patient ruler is dubbed "the long of breath" (25:15).

According to Robert Alden, the Hebrew word for temper in 14:29 refers to pliability in metal.[5] As pliability is a strength to metal, it is also a virtue to a person who must sometimes bend or flex in response to others. An ill-tempered person is one who is too unyielding. By remaining rigid, he breaks under pressure. Such persons can solve their anger problem by dealing with the underlying causes which could be "disappointment that life hasn't turned out as expected; desire to shore up a sagging self-image; guilt feelings; fear that if you bend a little you'll lose your convictions and morals."[6] In some respects, the ill-tempered person is like an addict. He or she obsessively tries to control the urge to rage and to be violent, knowing how frightening it is to be possessed by one's own anger. Like the alcoholic, he or she must give up efforts to control and, trusting God, must face anger in sensible, biblical ways.

GETTING TOUGH WITH ANGER

Check for a Cause

Angry Anatomy. It's wise to ask why anger is such a problem to you. Perhaps spiritual solutions have failed you because your problem is physical. A condition called hypoglycemia can pump huge amounts of adrenalin into the bloodstream. It's the powerful substance that preps the body to defend itself or deal with emergencies. A person with this chemical surging through his veins might be set off by the slightest annoyance. A person often spends years trying to cope with this condition through countless spiritual and self-help remedies, only to discover that all he needed to do was eat the right food at the right time.[7]

Since there are other physical causes, anyone gripped in an unusual struggle with ill-temper would be wise to consult a physician or psychiatrist.

The "B Factor". If anger's origin isn't in the body, it may be in the mind. One expert came into prominence a while ago by pointing out that we tend to bypass the mind in dealing with our emotions. He claims we typically look at an abusive situation as follows: "This makes me angry. I must control my anger to keep from hurting my child. But this child gets me so angry I can't control myself."

Albert Ellis analyzes this thinking to show us how we bungle our attempts to deal with anger. First, there is an antecedent event, "A." Randy goes to his toolbox for his screwdriver, finds it missing. "C" is the consequent emotion: Randy is furious. He stamps up the stairs yelling, "Whoever took my screw driver is going to get it." "D" stands for deeds. The deeds done in anger can be words or blows. "E" is for the end of the story. Possibly Randy apologizes later after he finds he left his screwdriver in the garage. Remorseful, he feels defeated by his lack of control. Unable to keep from getting angry, he concentrates on "D," the deeds, trying to keep from being destructive.

One major factor is left out of the formula, according to Ellis: "B." Between "A," the antecedent event and "C," the consequent emotion is the person's beliefs. Ellis also calls this a person's self-talk—what Randy says to himself that makes him get so angry. In this case, he could believe any number of things to justify intense anger. "Members of my family don't care, or they would return tools after they use them." "My wife isn't training the kids properly; if she were, they would put things away." His belief system turns a missing tool into something much bigger: his family's lack of love or his wife's failure as a mother. Once the molehill is transformed into a mountain, mountain-sized anger is the response. In addition, his belief system about anger kicks in. What

makes him think that even a huge problem calls for a big display of anger? Apparently, he is saying to himself that anger is the best, most appropriate response.

Examine what you are saying to yourself that makes you angry, Ellis advises. Then change your mind to make the anger unnecessary. Randy, for example, could start saying something like, "All of us make mistakes. The fact that the kids don't return tools is part of their immaturity; I will have to try harder to teach them to do so."

Here are some common beliefs behind the anger of adult children. "Unless I get angry to this degree, the kids won't listen to me." "Because she does this, it proves she doesn't love me." "The kids wouldn't behave like that if I were a better parent." "Unless I am angry, I won't do anything about this." "I have to get angry to keep people from taking advantage of me." "I am angry because I can't control this situation."

The Anger Advantage. Included in what you believe about anger are the thoughts about its rewards. Despite the fact that outbursts of anger can produce ugly results for which we are later sorry, we may believe there are some advantages to getting angry. These advantages break down into a number of types.

1) *The justice advantage.* You get angry because you feel an injustice is taking place—some goal or achievement is thwarted. Anger enables you to maintain the illusion that you are not giving in, you are continuing to fight for your own self-interest and are still in control. As long as you continue to stay angry, you feel you have not passively accepted defeat.[8]

A traffic jam is a good example. When a construction crew creates a long line of slow moving cars in front of us, there are two issues before us: control and trust. We cannot do anything about the situation, and we must trust those who have created it. An adult child can easily turn this into an occasion for anger, accusing the crew of gross injustice and stupidity. By getting upset we think we are doing something about the situation. Other motorists may sit there calmly allowing the construction to interfere with their lives, but we will not permit them to do so. If we give up our anger in such situations we look at it as giving up hope or giving in.

2) *The control advantage.* Since control seems to be such a major issue with adult children, we may use anger to help us get control and maintain it. We may have learned this from parents who used anger to get their own way with us. While anger is effective in getting others to obey, we need to lead in more positive ways.

3) *The self-justification advantage.* Anger can make us feel good about ourselves by blaming others for our predicament. Our own anger can be proof that we are right since we are convinced we wouldn't be angry if they weren't doing something wrong. Using uncalled-for anger to bolster our self-image is a poor substitute for healthier, more effective ways.

4) *The motivation advantage.* Anger is a great energizer. Some coaches use it to make their athletes perform better. Frank, an adult child of an alcoholic, was angry much of the time. A physician explained that he was using anger to motivate himself. As a child, he rarely obeyed his alcoholic father the first time he asked him to do something. It was only after he got mad at his dad's repeated nagging that he would go out and mow the lawn or clean his room. The doctor explained to him that as an adult he has to be angry to be motivated to do anything—hooked, in a sense, on his own adrenalin. Perhaps you are afraid to give up your anger because you'll lose your motivation. Like this adult child, you will have to treat your anger by learning to motivate yourself in other ways.

When you make a study of your anger, it's a good idea to keep a record for a month or two. Ask yourself, "When do I become angry?" "At whom?" "Why?" "What happened before I felt angry?" "How did I feel?" "What did I do when I was angry?" "How did people respond?" Look for patterns to your angry episodes. When you probe more carefully you will often see that anger isn't as much the problem as how you are using it. The key is not just to avoid an angry response, but to substitute another response in its place.

Send in a Substitute

Any number of emotions might be appropriate for a given situation. Caught in a traffic jam, late for work, some people will cry, others will explode. Those who blow their tops—especially adult children—may do so because they fear other emotions: sadness, disappointment, happiness, sensuality, etc. They substitute anger in their place. When a wife wants to get close to her husband, he may start a fight with her because he is scared of intimacy. A woman may get upset with the person who gets promoted instead of her because she can't stand feeling rejected, or she may become angry because she is disappointed.

Anger, then, can also be a cover-up for another emotion. Persons and events may not make you angry as much as the emotion the events cause. You get upset because you feel depressed, guilty, anxious, afraid or whatever. Sometimes anger is a good response to these feelings, but often there are healthier responses. Perhaps you become incensed with your spouse because you are deeply disappointed in yourself. Disappointment, then, is the underlying emotion you need to come to terms with. Discover what you are feeling when you are angry and deal with it.

We have already seen how adult children may react to people who control them. There's a logic to this since getting upset is normal when someone bugs you. The problem comes when you allow them to. In dealing with the habit of being taken advantage of, many adult children need to learn to stand up for themselves and their rights.

Accept Conflict

Bewildered, glancing at her husband, the woman spoke feelingly, "Why do we have this problem? We constantly differ over decisions. He wants to sell the extra refrigerator in the basement, I think we should keep it. I think we should paint the house this summer, he thinks we should wait. What's wrong with us?"

"Not a thing," I replied. My answer seemed to surprise her and her husband. "You look like two human beings to me, each with different temperaments and opinions. You have conflict for the same reason every other couple does: because you're married."

Sometimes adult children get mad because they don't accept conflict. Having seen so much of it, they may come to feel conflict itself is wrong, and when people bring it to them, they are unduly upset. Being a pleaser, I was like this. But I soon learned that a man can't be a good father if he can't welcome conflict; kids will always give it to you. This conflict is not the same as quarreling, which the Bible cautions us to avoid (Proverbs 17:14). "It is to a man's honor to avoid strife, but every fool is quick to quarrel" (Proverbs 20:3). Strife, however, isn't the same as conflict. Conflict occurs when we clash with someone over a difference of opinion or goal, etc. Quarreling and fighting are responses to conflict.

Friendships, partnerships, and marriages are mergers; when two people join together in some decision or activity, they should expect conflict. Being angry with someone just because they differ with you is like a woman being angry with her husband because he is a man. Differences—the stuff of relationships—should challenge instead of anger us. If we want to get close to people, conflict is a fact of life.

Verbalize Your Anger

I use the term *verbalize* to distinguish it from *express*. We can express anger in nonverbal ways: tone of voice, a slap, slamming the door. In part, we resort to violent and caustic expressions of temper because we want the person to know how we feel. Members of troubled families often don't do this because they don't accept their feelings. They have standard "don't feel, don't talk" rules. When miffed, you'll be surprised how an honest "I'm upset" takes the wind out of your sails. It pays to *verbalize* how you feel, to say "I'm very angry with you."

Deal with the Physical Effects of Anger

When the adrenal gland dumps its inflaming fluid into the arteries, things get hot in a hurry. To properly manage our temper we must watch our temperature. A biblical proverb warns us not to let the intensity rise in a conflict: "Starting a quarrel is like breaching a dam; so drop the matter before a dispute breaks out" (Proverbs 17:14). We may need to walk away when we're about to lose our cool. In fact, before discussing something that has angered us, we could have a more even temper by taking the proverbial "walk around the block" to work out some of the charged-up blood in our system.

DEPRESSIVE DEALINGS

The Slough of Despond

Watch out for the marshland of despair called depressive illness, different from more ordinary bouts of depression. From time to time we all have a lack of energy, a negative self-image, a sense of hopelessness, and other signs of depression. We can usually point to a clear-cut cause: an illness, exhaustion from hard work, a loss. A plunge to the emotional cellar may be common even when some event doesn't drop you there. A simple lack of exercise may be the culprit, or, for many women, physical changes prior to their monthly period. We can, however, separate between these so-called "normal," temporary bouts and more serious depression, though there are some similarities.

Depression is more serious if it prevents a person from functioning as normal for a period of time. While normal depression might keep a person off the job for a while (especially during periods of grief), the more serious variety might prevent a person from pulling his or her weight long after we would expect that person to snap out of it.

A Map of the State of Depression

"Why is light given to those in misery, and life to the bitter of soul?" (Job 3:20). Depression is one of the most common results of anger. To grapple with it, you need to recognize its symptoms. Job, the famous sufferer, describes his depression so accurately that you can use it to examine yourself.

Sleep disturbance. "When I lie down I think, `How long before I get up?' The night drags on, and I toss til dawn" (7:4).

Pessimism. "Man born of woman is of few days and full of trouble" (14:1).

Life seems worthless. ". . . I have no concern for myself; I despise my own life" (9:21).

Helplessness. "What I feared has come upon me . . . I have no rest, but only turmoil" (3:25, 26).

Physical signs of sadness. "My eyes have grown dim with grief; my whole frame is but a shadow" (17:7).

Desire for death. "To those who long for death that does not come, who search for it more than for hidden treasure" (3:21). Depression may also be marked by feelings of failure, lack of satisfaction, irritation, and loss of interest in people.

GETTING ON TOP OF BEING DOWN

A Chemical Connection

Since depression of any type can have a physical cause, adult children should be careful not to be misled about their depression. The connection between depression and childhood may seem so obvious that physical causes are ruled out, as was the situation of a woman who recently came to me for help. Throughout her more than five decades of life, she had often been so disabled by depression that she sat helplessly, unable to do her housework for months at a time. Now, she was viciously criticizing her husband, making life unbearable for him. Her childhood contained a clue: Her mother had dominated her and her father, sometimes hitting him with a skillet.

Prior to counseling with her, I sent her to a psychiatrist for a physical examination. He uncovered a chemical deficiency in her brain, prescribed the appropriate medicine, and two weeks later she was a different person. It turned out that her mother was responsible for her problem in an unsuspected way: She had genetically passed on the chemical deficiency.

This could be true of many adult children, whose dysfunctional parent acted the way he or she did because of a physical problem. An alcoholic's drinking or an abuser's angry outbursts may have been triggered by a depressive illness caused by a fault in the brain cells. A competent psychiatrist can help you find the truth if you suspect this may be so.

Good Grief

Some experts claim adult children go through a *repressed subterranean grieving process.*[9] This grandiose term means that deep down they are grieving over their childhood losses. Anger, guilt, and other emotions overtake them because they have not properly grieved over their disappointments. From this perspective it is the refusal to "bury them once and for all" that condemns adult children of alcoholics to live as prisoners of their pasts.

If true, this could explain the adult child's proneness to depression, since sadness is grief reaction. Reading this book may have started you mourning your losses even if your parents are still living. You may feel down, weepy, and deeply pained because of what you didn't have—encouraging words from a caring father, hugs from a warm mother, etc. According to these experts, you need to grieve for your losses.

Scripture also encourages Christians not to resist grieving (Acts 20:36-38; Philippians 2:27; 1 Peter 1:6). Permit your emotions to flow as you think about, talk about, and examine your childhood. An array of feelings appropriate to the stages of grief will surface: disappointment, sadness, anger, guilt, fear, anxiety. Don't fight them. Experience them and eventually they will give way to a calm acceptance of the past.

Sing the Blues

People with someone to confide in cope better with stress and depression. Despair thrives when kept hidden. Admitting to others your honest feelings keeps you honest with yourself and somehow opens holes to let out the gloom.

Thoughtful Feelings

Self-talk like, "I'm no good," or "I can't do anything right," or "God could never forgive my sin" isn't really what the intellect is saying; it's what the emotions are telling the intellect. When we remind ourselves that negative feelings give birth to negative thoughts, we can refuse to take those thoughts seriously.

When depression is an illness, a person is unable to control his thoughts and mistakenly takes them at face value. Normally, though, our thoughts can influence our feelings. We need to utilize our spiritual and mental resources when we are feeling blue by filling our minds with positive thoughts, even though the emotions are saying, "That's baloney." Words about hope, grace, love, and forgiveness may not immediately pop us into heavenly sunshine, but their input is significant in the long run.

Asking the Will to Help

Action is medicinal. Emotions respond to circumstances even when they don't respond to our thoughts. Emotions don't usually take orders like, "Stop feeling sad," or "Stop being angry." But when we feel blue we can ask our will to do something about it.

Psychologist William James maintained that our emotions are closely connected to our actions. We are afraid, he would say, because we are acting frightened. We are lazy because we are doing lazy things. Ever lie by a swimming pool thinking you ought to go in the water, but feeling like it's the last thing on earth you want to do? Somehow you manage to pull yourself up and jump in. In a few moments, you feel like swimming. James would explain that you feel like swimming because you are swimming. That reverses the usual notion—that we swim because we feel like it. We could help ourselves out of depression by doing nondepressive things—even if we don't feel like it.

The great reformer Martin Luther suggested some down-to-earth ways of coping with depression. He advised people with mild bouts to ignore the heaviness, shun solitude, and seek the warm company of friends. "A good way to exorcise the Devil," he also maintained, "[is] to harness the horse and spread manure on the fields."[10]

When depression makes us viciously turn on ourselves, we need to remind ourselves of this radical idea: "I did nothing to make God love me and I can do nothing to make Him love me less." In your hopeless state, hope in Him. The psalmist, depressed, spoke to himself in this way: "Why are you downcast, O my soul? Why so disturbed within me? Put your hope in God" (Psalm 42:5).

STANDING UP TO FEAR

Fear's Dreadful Face

Their welfare often in jeopardy, adult children are understandably familiar with fear. A reaction to danger, fear sets off all kinds of things in the body: a rapid and unusually strong heartbeat, quick or shallow breathing, trembling, sweating, muscular tension, dryness of the mouth, changes in voice quality, and faintness.[11]

We need to distinguish between feeling fear and acting in fear. Emotional fear occurs when we perceive a danger. Nothing seems to be wrong about feeling afraid when it alerts us to danger, just as pain warns us about physical problems. The psalmist David accepted his fear: "When I am afraid, I will trust in you" (Psalm 56:3). A

Christian should not expect to live a fearless life. Being afraid is not sinful, but reacting to fear can be.

We are sometimes put in a place where we must obey God or obey our fear. When we listen to our fear and acknowledge its mastery over us, this is sometimes okay. If you back away from a rattlesnake, you are showing due respect, a wise action. But whenever we fear something God has told us not to, and we back away from His will, we are giving more respect to what we fear than to God. Then fear competes with faith. Jesus said that ultimately we should "fear him which is able to destroy both soul and body in hell" (Matthew 10:28, KJV). In a sense, fear dethrones God.

When our fears are beyond reason, they become especially troubling to us as well as to those around us, especially when there is nothing to fear. Joan, an adult child, says she is afraid to drive a car. Further discussion discloses that she is afraid to take the driving test. Sitting beside a stranger who is about to pass judgment on her terrifies her so much that her husband is unable to persuade her to try it. She claims her fear is due to a grouchy driver's education teacher she had in high school. Yet the origin probably goes back even further. Her father divorced her mother and left when she was eight years old, and now the thought of rejection horrifies her, making her back away from any situation that might set her up for it.

Fear is a problem whenever our reaction to it is excessive. It's normal to be cautious about germs, avoiding close contact with someone with the flu or washing hands before eating. But I know a woman who, once a week, takes down all the curtains of her bedroom and washes them, the windows, and the windowsills. She turns over the mattresses weekly and vacuums them. She has little social life because so much of her time is spent in housecleaning. She has also tried to foist these same habits on her children, creating fears and conflicts within them.

Like us, this woman might get some relief from her obsessive fear by identifying it as an unnecessary, irrational piece of her past. In addition, there are practical approaches to fear that work.

GETTING THE BEST OF FEAR

Facing What You Fear

Fear prospers in isolation. The only way to shrink fear is to expose it to what scares you. You may be thinking, "What you say is the answer is really the problem. I can't face what frightens me because I'm too scared." Two suggestions can turn this thinking around. The first has to do with courage, a virtue of God's people in both the Old and New Testaments (Joshua 1:7; 1 Corinthians 16:13; 2 Corinthians 5:6). Courageous people are not the same as brave ones. Brave people are those who can face danger because they have no fear; courageous people face it in spite of their fear. Perhaps you've been asking God to make you brave by taking away your fear of something; instead, you might ask him to make you courageous, enabling you to face it.

The second suggestion has to do with how you face it. Getting closer by degrees is standard treatment for sexual dysfunctions. Couples are asked to refrain from intercourse and do less threatening things like giving backrubs, slowly progressing over a course of days or weeks to more intimate physical contact as the troubled partner's fears subside. Other fears can be handled in the same way. If possible, start with less threatening exposure like reading about the situation, and then move on as the fear lessens. Joan could begin by reading about driver's education, and then she could visit a driver's testing center and talk to those who give the tests.

Be Careful When You Let It Take Charge

It is because of our fears that we adult children often overreact. A woman whose parents divorced may be so afraid of a marital breakup that she goes to pieces over the slightest fracas with her husband. The adult child of an alcoholic will often have an excessive fear of alcohol. Think of his reaction the first time he smells beer on his teenager's breath.

Because we adult children have a tough time knowing what is normal, we should expect to be confused about our fears. It's not always easy to distinguish between what is legitimate and what is excessive. Yet we should be careful not to act out of fear by letting our fears dominate us. "God did not give us a spirit of timidity, but a spirit of power, of love and of self-discipline" (2 Timothy 1:7).

REPLACING ANXIETY

Anxious Agitations

Anxiety is part of the human condition. Psychologists call it general anxiety or "theological anxiety." One writer describes it in near poetic terms: "We are not completely comfortable with the stuff of our lives; things, jobs, relationships. We know that rust consumes, thieves break through and steal, the bell tolls. It may toll for a friend, a spouse, for me. I am . . . tomorrow I may not be."[12]

Anxiety is a painful emotional state marked by disquiet, alarm, or dread. A high degree of it can shorten one's attention span, hinder one's performance skills, interfere with problem solving, and prevent good communication.

Adult children may suffer from a less common form of anxiety. They have exaggerated feelings of helplessness and dread, even when there is no danger present or when the threat is mild.

Distinguishing genuine concern from needless anxiety is difficult, especially when adult children have loved ones in potentially disastrous situations. They are hard pressed to stop worrying about what accident a drunken parent might have or what harm he or she might do to a brother or sister still living at home.

Calming Your Qualms

In the New Testament, the term translated "anxiety" has several meanings. Sometimes it means undue concern, what we normally think of as worry. At other times, it merely describes a concern. Paul said that Christians should be concerned for each other and that he faced daily pressure of concern for all the churches (1 Corinthians 12:25, 2 Corinthians 11:28). Yet, using the same word, he commands, "Be anxious for nothing" (Philippians 4:6). Making the distinction between normal concern and worry will always be a problem for us. When someone says, "You worry too much," we may think we were only showing concern. At other times we condemn ourselves because we are too worried. This compounds the problem. We begin to worry about worrying. Our anxiety has anxiety.

We can help ourselves by accepting that it's okay to have "realistic concern." Lovingly, we can carry a burden for others that will drive us to pray for them or attempt to do something for them. We will never completely avoid the pain we feel on behalf of others, yet we should not allow it to severely distract or disable us.

You may have already begun to think differently about your anxiety because you have traced it to your childhood life of fear. If not, there are things you can do about it.

Apprehend Your Apprehensions. Make a study of yourself as a worrier. As with anger, seek answers to the questions: "What do I worry about?" "Does anything seem to trigger my anxiety attacks?" "When do I worry?" "How do I feel when I worry?" "How do I react when I worry?" "What usually helps me out of it?" It's possible that you will see a pattern to your anxiety. You may see your fear of certain things as a response to anxiety over security. Your fear of things like violent weather, crime, illness, may center around the threat of being abandoned or losing your self-esteem.

Inner conflict may also be a basic source of anxiety. Deep down inside, you are afraid to make decisions. Unmet needs may make you anxious. You feel something is missing and life is incomplete because your sexual, emotional, or social needs are not being met. If you can see a pattern to your anxiety, you can do things to reduce it.

Toss It Up. The apostle Peter instructs, "Cast all your anxiety on him because he cares for you" (1 Peter 5:7).

Since the Greek word for *cast* was commonly used to speak of tossing loads on donkeys, Peter suggests we throw our cares on God instead of carrying them ourselves. In fact, since he puts anxiety in the singular, he means for us to not only toss the things we worry about, but our worry as well.

The apostle Paul seems to suggest that we will never get rid of our anxiety entirely, but that we will constantly need God's help in dealing with it. "Be anxious for nothing," he writes, "but in everything by prayer and supplication with thanksgiving let your requests be made known to God. And the peace of God, which surpasses all comprehension, shall guard your hearts and your minds in Christ Jesus" (Philippians 4:6-7, NASB). The original Greek word for "guard" is used of placing a lid on a boiling pot. And so it is with the treatment of anxiety. The internal water boils, but a constant state of faith enables God's peace to come and put the lid on it. Pray about nothing and worry about everything; pray about everything and worry about nothing. Anxiety is not all bad; it will constantly drive us to God.

Share It. Telling others about your anxiety is so crucial, since loneliness only makes it worse. No human pain needs company as badly as anxiety. Being part of an open and honest group will help you know you are not alone in your anxiety and will help you carry your heavy burdens.

No matter what emotion most annoys us, we can eventually hope to feel better. We can also learn to feel better about ourselves, which is what we resolve to do next.

Notes

1. Patty McConnell, *Adult Children of Alcoholics: A Workbook for Healing* (San Francisco: Harper & Row, 1986).

2. O'Gorman and Oliver Diaz, p. 15.

3. Larry Crabb, *Understanding People* (Grand Rapids, Mich.: Zondervan, 1987), p. 69.

4. Peter H. Neidig and Dale H. Friedman, Spouse Abuse: A Treatment Program for Couples (Champaign, Ill.: Research Press Company, 1984), p. 74.

5. Robert Alden, *Proverbs: Commentary on an Ancient Book of Timeless Advice* (Grand Rapids, Mich.: Baker Book House, 1983), pp. 115-16.

6. Charles M. Sell, *House on the Rock: Wisdom from Proverbs for Today's Families* (Wheaton, Ill.: Victor Books, 1987), p. 125.

7. Richard Ecker, *The Stress Myth* (Downers Grove, Ill.: InterVarsity Press, 1985), pp. 126-31.

8. Neidig and Friedman, p. 81.

9. D. Frye, "Griefwork and the Adult Children of Alcoholic Families," *Children of Alcoholics Review* 10 & 11, pp. 8-12, cited by Sandra D. Wilson, p. 35.

10. Roland Bainton, *Here I Stand* (Nashville, Tenn.: Abingdon, 1950), p. 364.

11. John Altrocchi, *Abnormal Behavior* (New York: Harcourt, Brace, Jovanovich , 1980), p. 41.

12. Gordon Jackson, "Anxiety and the Church's Role," *Journal of Religion and Health* 14 (no. 4, 1975): 231.

RESOLVE

We will face any shame we got from our past and become less critical and more positive about ourselves.

9

Forming a Better Self-Image

A dult children from dysfunctional homes are not the only ones who struggle with low self-esteem. When asked, most adults will say they also struggle, causing experts to suspect that many people think they have a lower self-esteem than they really have. It's important to understand what low self-esteem is so that we can determine the extent of it in our own lives. Look for the following symptoms as outlined by David Carlson.[1]

Fear of being known. There is little inner peace for someone who deep down is ashamed of who he is and is afraid others will find out. "I often turn myself off to people who want to get to know me better. My whole insides shake when I talk to them. My self-esteem has been so bad that I've thought I was bothering people when I talked to them." Though Mike is in his mid-twenties, his fears match those of a thirteen-year-old. "I always felt like people were laughing at me. I have always felt like a walking joke, and though I was hurting very badly inside, I acted as if nothing was wrong. If I told someone how I felt and opened myself up to them, the possibility that they would laugh at me would be too much to bear."

Blurred sense of self and others. An ACoA describes how he experienced this. "Suppose someone has just had a bad day and is tense. If that person was short with me, or made a bad remark to me, even if it was not the truth, I would assume I was wrong, even though I wasn't." Once again, co-dependency shows its face, this time as a problem of self-esteem. The sense of self is so small, the co-dependent can't distinguish what he feels from what others feel. When the alcoholic is depressed, his co-dependent is depressed. Thus, he doesn't even know what he is feeling because his feelings don't matter. Maybe if he really thought about it, the co-dependent might realize he's really angry. But it would be far too threatening to his small ego to tell that to the alcoholic father, so he goes through life without admitting to himself or others how he really feels.

Difficulty accepting compliments and criticism. If your inner self is about as tall as a blade of grass, any criticism can tear it down to nothing. Even a friendly suggestion for improvement will almost knock you over. It would seem that good feedback, like a compliment, would build you up. But as long as you can't see any good in yourself, the person who tries to point some out is either a fool, a liar, or just trying to be nice. Anyway, you're so downright self-conscious, you're uncomfortable. One adult child admitted, "I felt really bad most of the time and didn't know why. I felt nervous around others because I didn't know what they thought about me. I was unsure about myself, about what I should do, how I should feel. I put a tremendous importance upon what others thought of me."

Unable to let others be themselves. This comes from a blurred sense of personal boundaries. People with a fragile sense of self are threatened by getting close to people who are different from them, people who don't conform to their own image of themselves. If they are insecure about their Christian faith, they may have trouble befriending a Hindu. Afraid they might lose what they have, they've got to defend it fiercely. This defense is not the same as a good, clear, convincing witness for Christ. Rather, it is an arrogant, selfish disrespect of the right of other people to be themselves so long as they are not violating anyone else's rights. Even people with low self-esteem can be proud.

Unable to celebrate successes and mourn losses. Feeling great about a job well done is ruled out if you don't accept yourself because you envy someone with a better job. Jealousy keeps us from rejoicing with those who rejoice over their accomplishments. Having so little to lose, we deny our losses and excuse our failures, or else we are so devastated by them that we stay angry or depressed for long periods. For some, self-pity is an excuse to do drugs or hit the bottle.

Inability to distinguish "no" from rejection. People with low self-esteem are clingers. They will sacrifice to get a relationship going and then hang on tightly. They feel discarded if someone cancels a lunch date . . . destroyed if someone ends a love affair. When they project these feelings on others, they are labeled possessive.

Unable to let go of a negative past. Low self-esteem breaks out in a severe case of "could-have-beens." Because they blame the past for their present state, they always want to change it. Past mistakes and failures are hard to let go of. People with low self-esteem can't seem to realize the past can't be changed, undone, or made up for.

Unable to compromise during conflict. The struggle with compromise is related to the inability to allow others to be themselves. To compromise we must hold on to our values and integrity, and allow others to keep theirs without either of us losing ourselves. People with little self-worth can't easily do this; they see issues as either black or white.

Unable to care for a person without rescuing them. Carlson offers these questions to determine whether you are a rescuer or a mere helper: "Can I help you only as much as you ask for and need it? When I am helping you, how frequently do I feel like a victim? Can I help you without blaming you or feeling blamed?"[2]

Unable to maintain confidentiality. A person with little self-worth may gossip about other people's weaknesses to make himself look better.

You need not have a major problem with all ten of these items to suffer from a problem of self-worth. Whatever you may have a problem with, you'll need to turn negative statements into positive ones. Instead of saying, "I can't celebrate my successes," you need to shout, "I am going to learn to celebrate!" Instead of saying, "I can't compromise," say, "I am going to risk compromising."

HOW I WOULD LOOK WITH SELF-ESTEEM

Based on what experts say about self-esteem, I have written the following profile of a person who has it:

A person with a good self-esteem will be able to give and receive affection freely, able to receive a compliment and give it. Resisting social pressures to reform, she will have confidence in her own ideas and values. She can detect when something is wrong and is a threat and won't run headlong into harmful suggestions like taking drugs.

She will be able to solve problems creatively with some degree of confidence, play an active role in social groups. When asked, she can identify her strengths as well as weaknesses and expresses her views frequently and effectively. She will choose personal goals that are risky, but not foolishly beyond her ability to pursue. Her plans and objectives will be based on present performance and not some dreamy ideal: "Someday, I'll make it big," or "Someday, I'll minister to millions of people."

You won't hear a lot of anxious talk from her—like, "I'll never succeed; that will never work." Nor will you see too many signs of self-doubt, like her putting off too long the making of a decision. Close relationships will be no problem with her. She won't always be saying "I'm sorry," endlessly apologizing even when there is nothing to be sorry about. She may or may not enjoy being around people, but she won't run from social obligations. Inside she won't be filled with false guilt, depression and shame. She enjoys her successes, feels important and worth something to God and to others.[3]

IS SELF-ESTEEM CHRISTIAN?

Research has shown that high self-esteem is an indication of mental health.[4] Yet some Christians dispute this. They claim non-Christian psychologists put too much stress on self-esteem, and when they test for it, they use non-Christian values and beliefs. For example, many tests rate a person high in self-esteem if he feels good about his actions. Such tests may show less self-esteem in a Christian since he is more sensitive to sin. This raises a few questions: "Is a Christian concept of self-esteem different from a non-Christian one?" "Doesn't Scripture commend self-sacrifice, not self-love?" "Doesn't Christian humility require a dim view of ourselves?" "Isn't today's self-esteem grounded in self-worship and pride?"

However we answer these questions, there is no biblical warrant for a Christian feeling rejected, worthless, and ashamed. The following guidelines can help us adult children develop a more positive picture of ourselves.

A MATTER OF WORTH

Estimate your worth in God's eyes. Self-esteem includes self-love. At first, this term may sound suspicious to the Christian, whose life is built on two commandments: to love the Lord your God with all your heart and with all your soul and with all your mind and to love your neighbor as yourself (Matthew 22:37, 38). In addition, Jesus says, "If anyone would come after me, he must deny himself and take up his cross daily and follow me. For whoever wants to save his life will lose it, but whoever loses his life for me will save it" (Luke 9:23-24). Self also takes second place to others, for Paul writes, "In humility consider others better than yourselves" (Philippians 2:3).

Clearly, the Christian is to live unselfishly. But properly understood, self-love is not selfishness. Self-worth is implied in the command to love your neighbor as yourself. We are to love others because they are of worth, just as we are. When Paul tells us to consider others better than ourselves, he doesn't ask us to deny our own needs. He says in the following verse, "Each of you should look not only to your own interests, but also to the interests of others" (Philippians 2:4). Paul is attacking "selfish ambition and vain deceit," not self-regard.

The worth of every human being is a cardinal doctrine of Christian faith, built on the fact that every person is created in the image of God. This is why murder is so terrible (Genesis 9:6). This is why James condemns cursing another human being (James 3:3-9). Why then should I curse myself?

Nothing should rob us of our sense of worth, not even our most terrible sins, failures, or faults. The fall of mankind did not destroy the fact that we are created in the image of God (Genesis 9:6; James 3:9). It is because of human worth that Christians take such a serious view of sin.

Own Your Own Self-image

Margaret is like many of us. She was convinced that until she could get her father to love her she would never feel good about herself. Whenever you place your standard of approval outside yourself, you are in trouble. It means that you must seek to win that approval; it depends on someone else. You are trapped, victimized. "I am not what I think I am; I am not what you think I am; I am what I think you think I am."

Start by recognizing that your self-image is your own. You are the one who sets the standards for self-approval. If you have decided that the approval of someone else is necessary before you feel worth, then you will always be looking outside of yourself for approval.

Now, I'll grant you that God has His standards, and we'll discuss those in a moment. But not all our standards must be those others have for us. If that were so, we couldn't obey God. The apostle Paul wrote, "I care very little if I am judged by you or by any human court; indeed, I do not even judge myself. My conscience is clear, but that does not make me innocent. It is the Lord who judges me" (1 Corinthians 4:3, 4). In another place he affirms his freedom from others: "Am I now trying to win the approval of men, or of God? Or am I trying to please men? If I were still trying to please men, I would not be a servant of Christ" (Galatians 1:10).

Ask yourself what expectations you keep reinforcing to yourself. Are you saying things like you won't be satisfied until you accomplish such and such? Perhaps these messages came from your parents. However, they are now yours, and you have the power to change them.

Don't Try to Prove Self-worth

In the past I've tried to prove my own worth instead of accepting it. This is the plight of the co-dependent whose sense of self is so wrapped up in externals (if we can get people to say good words, award us diplomas and badges and awards, we can begin to feel like we are something). Contemporary society promotes this idea. James Dobson popularized this idea in his book about building our children's self-esteem. Because our society makes us feel good about ourselves only when we are making a contribution, we should give each child the chance to excel in playing baseball, blowing a trumpet, running a computer, etc. This is sound advice. Yet such accomplishments are not the major basis for self-worth.

What we make of ourselves, by God's grace, plays a part in our self-esteem, but it is not the primary basis. We can never do enough to establish our true worth. That worth comes from God, our creator. Compare a person to a gold necklace and you'll see better what I mean. A gold necklace has worth because it is a necklace, but it has a prior worth because it is gold. Humans are like that: No matter what shape we are in, we are precious simply because we exist. Sin doesn't ruin our self-worth.

In the earlier years of my ministry I used to think of myself and others as having worth only because Christ saved us. In a conference in the mountains of California I told a group of college students, "Be honest with others, because you have nothing to lose; you are nothing to begin with." I quoted Paul's words: "Neither he who plants nor he who waters is anything, but only God. . ." (1 Corinthians 3:7). We were just a piece of junk lying around when Christ came to save us.

After my speech, a Christian psychologist who had been in the audience came up to me, peered down, and angrily said, "Never again tell these people they are nothing." Then he quoted Francis Schaeffer's words: "Man is sinful, but he is not junk." I was dumbstruck; what could I say? He was absolutely right. I slipped back to my cabin as quickly as I could to permit the red to fade from my face and to set my own thinking straight. Even though I had a degree in theology, my thinking was faulty. Worth isn't found in our accomplishments, nor in our salvation, but in something that comes prior to those two: our creation. We have worth because God has created us. That is why God sent Christ to save us: because He loved us. That day I said to myself, "I have worth just sitting here in this cabin doing nothing."

That moment my attitude toward myself changed. It didn't end my battle with self-esteem, but the urgency to prove myself began to disappear. I felt a new inner strength. Prior to this I was like a house built on the wrong foundation. Now I have a solid foundation that neither the winds of failure nor the storms of sin can move. No matter how much I fail, how little I accomplish, how much I sin, I have worth. No one and nothing can touch this; not shame, not a parent's or others' criticisms, not guilt or failure.

SELF-RESPECTING SINNERS

There is more to self-esteem than a sense of worth. We should also do things to enhance our self-respect, which is a bit different from self-worth. Experts say that our self-respect comes from comparing our perceived self and our ideal self. The closer we think we are to what we wish we were, the more self-respect we will have.

Perfectionism: Who Needs It?

We can't base our self-esteem on doing God's will, because we all fall short of it. Self-esteem has to be built on forgiveness, not perfection. Perfectionism is a special problem for adult children. We fantasize about the way we would like to be to make up for the way we are. We may have learned this from a parent who did the same. Talk to an alcoholic sometime and you'll discover a person full of dreams: Someday he'll have that big house by the lake; someday she'll earn that master's degree in ꞈomputer science.

We have to face our perfectionism for what it is: pride. When we set our own standards, we fashion ourselves as gods. This, according to the great theologian Augustine, is the very root of all sin. Said the apostle Paul, we "exchanged the glory of the immortal God for images made to look like mortal man" (Romans 1:23). Human nature seeks nothing more than to be flattered. So many of us seem to have problems with self-esteem, but whenever we are tested, the great majority of us think we are better than average; we perceive ourselves as more intelligent and more sociable than our peers.

A college board recently invited the million high school seniors who took its aptitude test to indicate "how you feel you compare with other people your own age in certain areas of ability." It appears that American high school seniors are not racked with inferiority feelings.

While 60 percent reported themselves as better than average in athletic ability, only 6 percent felt themselves to be below average. In leadership ability, 70 percent rated themselves as above average, 2 percent below average. In ability to get along with others, 0 percent of the 829,000 students who responded rated themselves below average, 60 percent rated themselves in the top 10 percent, and 25 percent saw themselves among the top 1 percent.[5]

David Meyers, professor of Hope College in Michigan, puts it bluntly: "Most of us are not groveling about with feelings that everyone else is better than we are." What, then, causes the loss of self-esteem? We judge ourselves to be better than we are and feel bad that we are not.

A Sober Approach to Self-Esteem

True humility is more like self-forgetfulness than modesty. In Romans 12 the apostle Paul gave sound advice: "For by the grace given me I say to every one of you: Do not think of yourself more highly than you ought, but rather think of yourself with sober judgment, in accordance with the measure of faith God has given you." Oddly, low self-esteem can come from thinking too highly of ourselves. To stop this, we have to see how our attempt to be better than we are is a strategy that comes from our childhood. In the past, we may have decided to be better than our parents and those around us as a way of feeling less a part of such a messed up family.

It's futile to try to feel good about yourself by being better than your parents; part of how you feel about yourself has to do with your parents. The shame we feel for them, we will feel for ourselves. Instead of comparing our goodness with their badness, we need to try to see their strengths, doing our best to have a proper image of them. Not only will this shore up our own self-image, it will put us in a better position to relate to them. Taking the pressure off ourselves will help us take it off others.

Failure: Why Not?

One of the lies perfectionism whispers in our ears is, "You really shouldn't sin." When we do, we have a terrible time with ourselves. This is not to say we shouldn't feel bad for sinning, but, having confessed our sin, we should be willing to forgive ourselves as God has forgiven us.

One man told me how he scolded his child more severely than he should have. In a more sober moment, he recognized what he had done and was overcome with guilt and depression. In tears he asked his son to forgive him. But he couldn't forgive himself, dejectedly dragging himself around for days. Noticing his condition, a friend asked what was wrong. The friend offered this advice: "You should be glad this happened; you taught your son a major lesson. From you he learned how we should confess to someone after we have wronged them."

Only then did he begin to feel better about himself. Yet notice how his perfectionism kept him from forgiving himself in the first place. Until his friend told him some good would come from the episode, he couldn't accept his failure. He needed something positive to come from the negative.

Not every sin can be an occasion for good. Sometimes we simply have to see ourselves as someone who can do wrong and be wrong. But we must also learn to mourn our losses and our failures and move on.

Sinner? Yep

This doesn't mean we skip over our sinfulness to maintain our self-respect. Scripture tells us that while we have worth, we also sense our own unworthiness. As

Isaiah did, it's healthy to sometimes cry out, "Woe to me! . . . I am ruined! For I am a man of unclean lips, and I live among a people of unclean lips, and my eyes have seen the King, the LORD Almighty" (Isaiah 6:5). Becoming a Christian includes stripping away our defenses and denial and taking an honest look at ourselves.

Christian self-esteem isn't based on thinking there is nothing wrong with us. We can see ourselves as sinners and still have a sense of our worth and God's love for us. I can respect my basic self and still not like some of the parts of what I am. Self-esteem says that I have strengths, I have potential. I can like some of what I find in myself. The bad doesn't wipe out what's right about me.

Scripture clearly tells Christians how to deal with sin and still keep self-respect. We are told to confess it and believe God has forgiven it (1 John 1:9). Confession is the Christian's safety valve. If we weren't able to confess, we would be overwhelmed by pent-up guilt because Christian standards are high. "Be perfect, therefore, as your heavenly Father is perfect" (Matthew 5:48). Confessing means admitting. When we admit we've broken a standard, we recognize the standard exists. When we admit we've come short of the glory of God, we affirm there is a glorious God.

One of my seminary teachers, Haddon Robinson, once told a joke to make this point. A man entered a bar, bought a glass of beer and then immediately threw it into the bartender's face. Quickly grabbing a napkin, he helped the bartender dry his face while he apologized with great remorse. "I'm so sorry," he said. "I have this compulsion to do this. I fight it, but I don't know what to do about it." "You had better do something about your problem," the bartender replied. "You can be sure I'll remember you and will never serve you another drink until you get help."

It was months before the man faced the bartender again. When he asked for a beer, the bartender refused. Then the man explained that he had been seeing a psychiatrist and that his problem was solved. Convinced it was now okay to serve him, the bartender poured him a drink. The man took the glass and splashed the beer into the barkeeper's astonished face. "I thought you were cured," the shocked bartender screamed. "I am," said the man. "I still do it, but I don't feel guilty about it anymore."

People who can't see God as forgiving maintain their self-respect and dissolve their guilt by lowering their standards or giving them up altogether. Christians are also tempted to do this, but owning up to our shortcomings is a better way. When we break the lofty standards of Scripture, we can still feel okay about ourselves by falling on 1 John 1:9: "If we confess our sins, He is faithful and just to forgive us our sins."

Overcoming Sin? Uh-huh

Besides confessing our sins, we ought to pray and work to overcome them. In search of mental health we sometimes disconnect our feelings from our actions. A wife of a young attorney was making a name for herself in the community. Her life consisted of a round of community activities. Suddenly, she lost her vitality and began to drop out of all social events. She was unable to sleep and had lost her appetite. She summed up her problem for her doctor in one word: depression. Believing it was caused by chemical problems, he treated her accordingly. Still depressed, she consulted a Christian psychologist who uncovered her real problem: She was having an affair with a friend of her husband. The psychologist reported, "Guilt and bad feelings about herself had caught up with her. The deceit with her husband, the lies, the attempts to cover up, her own lack of sexual response to her husband—all these came to a head in emotional exhaustion and depression."[6]

Sometimes we are too hard on guilt. "Guilt feelings are not always bad," writes evangelical psychologist Gary Collins. "They can stimulate us to change our behavior." The apostle Paul valued the fear associated with guilt: "Those who continue in sin, rebuke in the presence of all, so that the rest also may be fearful of sinning" (1 Timothy 5:20, NASB). Also, it seems that we might feel quite bad about ourselves if we continue to betray God's standards. The Bible speaks of having a *good conscience* and of doing things "because of conscience." What we are feeling may be related to what we are doing. A Christian who is secretly committing adultery should not be surprised if his self-esteem is sagging a bit. This means that whenever we do conquer a problem, we are bound to feel better about ourselves. When we grow in grace, we will grow in self-esteem. This, of course, doesn't mean we have to be perfect to feel right about ourselves.

FEELING OK

We should practice all the standard approaches to feeling forgiven: regular confession of sin, memorization and review of verses about God's forgiveness, attendance at church meetings and communion services where there is group confession of sin and public assurance of God's grace. In the long run, these "spiritual" approaches should result in feeling at peace with God. Yet they don't always end this way, primarily because self-forgiveness is more than a spiritual issue for some people. It is an emotional one. We can know we are forgiven without feeling we are. There are approaches we can take to change this deeply-felt attitude toward ourselves.

False Guilt

First, we can refuse false guilt by making our mind an ally in battling our emotions. Sometimes this means that when we feel guilty after confessing our sins, we order this "false guilt" to scram. We should be careful not to call something sin that isn't.

We have already seen that adult children tend to be self-blamers, loading themselves with false guilt by turning right into wrong. When they become Christians they may take their failures even more seriously. False guilt may be a product of a legalistic childhood family. "In our Christian home, we had a rule for everything," said one man. "All the rules were connected to our faith in God, even things like when we went to bed. As an adult, I struggle daily with heavy guilt over things that just don't matter." While the Bible claims conscience sometimes plays a role in our lives (1 Timothy 1:5; 3:9), it warns us that it is not always reliable, being defiled and seared as with a branding iron (1 Corinthians 8:7; 1 Timothy 4:2).

Conscience has two ways of letting us down. Sometimes it will be as silent as a sleeping mouse when we are doing something terrible, like wrecking a person's reputation. Other times, when we are doing something perfectly all right, like enjoying some leisure time, it bellows like a roaring elephant. The only sure way to know when to pay attention to it is by knowing God's Word. Scripture not only tells us what is wrong so we can avoid it, it affirms what is right so we can enjoy it. "It is for freedom that Christ has set us free" (Galatians 5:1). We need to retrain our conscience by saying, "What I am now doing is okay. Go ahead and scream; you'll eventually stop." Granted, it usually won't be scared off that easily. But if we try hard to believe our heads instead of our hearts, "false guilt" will become more and more reluctant to show its face.

Negative Feelings: Share Them

As you share your past experiences with others, share the negative feelings you have about yourself. We didn't get our poor self-image alone; we probably won't change it alone. Others can help supply the approval we didn't get from our parents.

Sensitive friends can say good things about us to counter the bad we are used to hearing.

For most of my life people have been telling me not to be so hard on myself. It's taken me a long time to start listening to them. A support group can make us feel accepted even though our inner voices make it hard to accept ourselves. Here's how one man described how he benefited from our group:

While there are immense benefits to be gained from counseling, I believe I have gained more from my group. Group members have helped me more than almost anyone else in my life. It was scary at first. I was afraid I would talk too much or that others would not want to hear me or that perhaps I had no dysfunctional family background at all. Once I started to talk, though, the feelings of relief started to flow. The people I was with listened intently, and I felt that, at last, I could understand better why I am the way I am. Why do I always feel different? I now know that it is okay to be different. To have come from an alcoholic home was not my fault. Somewhere deep down inside I had been hiding false guilt. My group gave me affirmation, nurture, and love.

He compares the group to a parental role:

Besides parenting yourself, you allow others in the group to parent you. I have not yet understood this, but there is a tremendous amount of healing that comes from helping others to heal. The self-esteem built up from seeing others benefit from my advice is a big part of my healing. But having someone really, really know me and love me anyway has been the biggest part.

Truth: Meditate on It

Current research about our brains tells us the two halves function differently. Among other differences, the right side processes pictures while the left works with words. The way we remember people's faces provides a good example of how each side works. It's much easier to recognize someone when you see them again than it is to describe them to someone else. This is because the right side of the brain registers a portrait of them in your memory bank. If a policeman asks you to find a suspect in a book, you might be able to do so using the right side of your brain, even though your left side couldn't answer specific questions about hair color or clothes.

Besides having different functions, each side of the brain has a somewhat different doorway into it. Well-reasoned arguments get to the left side of the brain. Pictures will more likely make it into the right side. Your poor self-image is probably stored, in part, in the right side of your brain. In other words, you have this unconscious picture of yourself painted by numerous childhood experiences, some of them before you could even talk. All the input into the other side of the brain, the left side, doesn't seem to change it much. Good arguments like, "If Christ died for all our sins, He died for the ones I committed after accepting Him as well as the ones before," still don't help you feel forgiven. Biblical statements like, "Therefore, since we have been justified through faith, we have peace with God through our Lord Jesus Christ," don't seem to touch your guilt like they should. Perhaps this is because you are using left-brain approaches to what is a right-brain problem.

To change the right brain, you may need to think in pictures. Perhaps this is one of the reasons there are so many word pictures in the Bible. Try, for example, meditating on biblical passages that use word pictures. Isaiah assures God's people, "Though your sins are like scarlet, they shall be as white as snow" (Isaiah 1:18). Speaking of their wicked pasts, Paul tells the Christians of Corinth, "But you were washed" (1 Corinthians 6:11). Not only can we memorize and meditate on picturesque verses like these, but we can deliberately apply these pictures to ourselves when we feel bad about our failures and sins.

Sometimes it helps first to make a mental image of your bad feeling, whether it is shame, guilt, or dejection. For example, one man describes the depression he feels after failure as a warm, heavy glob of glue that pours down over him, dragging him down and suffocating his joy. Once you picture the negative feeling, you can formulate another picture to attack it. This man pictured a warm shower that dissolved and washed away the glue.

Keep the pictures and verses handy and meditate on them whenever the right side of your brain flashes its negative images on the screen of your mind.

FOCUS ON THE NEW IMAGE

The Christian has several positive images he can meditate on. In Christ, we are new creatures, who "have put on the new self, which is being renewed in knowledge in the image of its Creator" (Colossians 3:10). The New Testament describes vividly the traits of the new self as love, joy, peace, patience, kindness, goodness, faithfulness, gentleness, self-control, compassion, humility along with all of the other traits of Jesus Christ (Galatians 5:22-23; Colossians 3:12). Not only does the Bible tell us to "put these things on," but to picture ourselves as "having put on" (Colossians 3:10). Even though we fall short of this picture in practice, we are to maintain it in our minds. It is the position we have been given and the one to which we aspire. It gives us the right to think positively, which not only makes us feel better about ourselves today, but makes us do better with ourselves tomorrow.

Negative thinking is as damaging to us as positive thinking is beneficial. Maxwell Maltz, a plastic surgeon, discovered how crucial self-image was to his patients' recovery. Using his surgical skill, for example, he might straighten a man's deformed hand. Yet, after the surgery, the patient would still dangle the hand beside him as he had done when it was useless. Though his hand was no longer crippled, his mind thought it was.

Maltz tells the dramatic story of a woman who underwent several operations on her face. When Maltz removed the bandages from her face after the final surgery, he thought to himself, *How amazing is this art of plastic surgery; this woman is now attractive.* Excited, he held the mirror for her to see the results. Her response startled him: "I knew it would never work." Though her exterior image was pretty, her interior one was still ugly. To help her and others like her change their view of themselves after surgery, Maltz studied psychology. He then wrote the best-selling book *Psycho-Cybernetics* to explain how success for anyone begins with a positive attitude.

The apostle Paul taught this. "Since, then, you have been raised with Christ, set your hearts on things above, where Christ is seated at the right hand of God. Set your minds on things above, not on earthly things. For you died, and your life is now hidden with Christ in God. When Christ, who is your life, appears, then you also will appear with him in glory" (Colossians 3:1-4). We will become new because we are new. This doesn't mean that we forget the possibility of our sin, but that we focus on the potential of salvation.

Give It Up

When facing a challenge, say, "I can do it," instead of, "I'll never make it." When tackling a personal problem tell yourself, "By God's grace, I'll eventually overcome," instead of, "I'll be this way forever." When looking at one of your negative traits, replace "I am so compulsive" with "By the Holy Spirit's power, I am self-disciplined."

One of my favorite sports stories is about a boy named Walter. As a child, Walter was crippled by infantile paralysis. A doctor told Walter's mother her son would never walk. Refusing to believe this, she did everything she could to help him recover, endlessly massaging his legs and bathing them in warm water. Walter did walk, and eventually he ran. Watching a track meet at a high school one day, he said to himself, *I'm going to be the world's greatest high jumper*. He practiced, and when he got to high school he made the track team.

In college he continued his quest to excel in the high jump. When he would return home with severe pain in his legs, his wife would say, "Walter, you not only have strength in your legs; you have it in your heart." Together they talked of the power of faith—that if someone believed strongly enough in something they wanted to do, it would empower them.

Not long after that, Walter matched the world record for the high jump. The crowd hushed as the bar was lifted to 5 feet 11 and 3/4 inches. If he cleared it he would establish a new record. On the first try, Walter hit the bar and it tumbled down with him. It was the same on the second try. As he prepared to make his third and final jump, he tells us that he remembered what he and his wife had discussed about the strength of belief. As he started his approach, he pictured himself clearing the bar. The boy they said would never walk became world champion high jumper Walter Davis.

Try this yourself. Do you have an important social event tonight? Before you go, preview how you will behave, but be realistic. Don't imagine things you can't control. A positive attitude is not wishful thinking; it's getting your mind off the "can'ts" and onto the "cans," moving from "me, the failure" to "me, the victor."

CHOOSE REALISTIC GOALS

If people feel they are not measuring up to their ideals, they can do something to remedy their frustration. They can try harder to reach their goals, or they can change their goals. Some of us need to work less at achieving our goals and more at changing them.

We have already noted how adult children, fired by their own childhood fantasies, become perfectionists. They choose impossible goals for themselves and then cruelly judge themselves for not living up to them. Becoming a Christian may not change this. Now that we are in touch with a supernatural God, we may aim for even more, misusing Paul's words, "I can do everything through him who gives me strength" (Philippians 4:13). We can't do everything. We can face everything God wills for us, which is the meaning of Paul's statement.

To select life goals, we must add together our gifts, abilities, age, health, and opportunities. The apostle Paul explained, "Do not think of yourself more highly than you ought, but rather think of yourself with sober judgment, in accordance with the measure of faith God has given you" (Romans 12:3). Sober judgment requires thinking of ourselves no more or no less than we ought. Expecting too much devastates our self-esteem.

John Quincy Adams held more important offices than anyone else in the history of the United States. He served with distinction as president, senator, congressman, minister to major European powers, and participated in various capacities in the American Revolution, the War of 1812, and events leading to the Civil War. Yet, at age seventy, with much of that behind him, he wrote, "My whole life has been a succession of disappointments. I can scarcely recollect a single instance of success in anything that I ever undertook."[7] Such is the fate of those who base self-regard on attaining unrealistic ideals or surpassing the feats of others.

Laying aside our pretensions is as much of a relief as gratifying them. A wealthy ACoA had quite a lucrative job that robbed him of his family life, contentment, and Christian service. When he learned about the effects of growing up in an alcoholic home, he saw that his enormous ambition was linked to the pressure to succeed that his father had forced on him. Once he was aware of this, his desire to make money vanished. He has now chosen a job that ministers to people and gives him time to pursue other goals.

SET SOBER STANDARDS

I asked one of my former students what he had learned after his first year of ministry. "I have learned to be mediocre," he said. In the isolation of a seminary classroom, he got drunk on idealism. But a real church with real people in real life sobered him up.

Trusting God, we can only do our best and leave the miracles to Him. We learn to pray for "the serenity to accept the things we cannot change." If we connect our self-esteem too closely with being highly successful, we may find it unbearable to accept being average, which most of us are.

CELEBRATE YOUR SUCCESSES

In our support group we take little victories seriously. We get excited over reports like these: "I talked to my mom on the phone the other day and when I hung up I wasn't depressed as much as I used to be." "I'm still angry with my dad, but last week I was able to say with some meaning, `I love you.' " Even the smallest step is a giant step if it's in the right direction. God isn't just concerned with how far we've come, but where we are headed. We need to be glad for any degree of progress and not wait until we have solved the whole problem before we accept ourselves. To do otherwise is to continue to do what was done in our childhood. We need to be a more sympathetic parent to ourselves by getting high on our victories, even the small ones.

There are some practical ways to do this. First of all, share your victories with others who understand. Report the smallest step of progress. Second, treat yourself like you would treat a friend. Suppose, for example, you risked a change in your behavior and ended up with 80 percent failure and 20 percent success. Ask yourself how you would respond to a friend who did that. Those of us with low self-esteem are thousands of times harsher with ourselves than we are with our friends. Try balancing that out; be as good a friend to yourself as you are to others.

Third, we can learn to celebrate in a variety of ways. Celebration doesn't always include having a party or rewarding ourselves with a pizza. But most adult children need to learn to give themselves a treat without feeling guilty about it. We can also find a quiet place and sing a praise chorus or read a psalm of victory. We can put a gold star on our calender and find other creative ways to honor what we are accomplishing instead of always lamenting what we are not.

SEEK SELF-FULFILLMENT

Jesus promised that his disciples would find their lives by losing them. This is what self-fulfillment is: discovering our place and purpose in the will of God. To His followers He promised "abundant life."

Self-fulfillment is selfish when all we pursue is our own welfare and concerns. Yet there is nothing wrong with getting a deep sense of satisfaction from our jobs and other personal pursuits. We need to avoid the extreme suggestion that the only time a Christian can feel fulfilled is when he or she is acting unselfishly. This is what traps the co-dependent, who denies self to a fault and does so more because of contempt of self than love of others. Why help others enjoy life if we are not to enjoy it ourselves? Why devote our lives to meeting other people's needs without allowing them to meet ours?

There are numerous ways to feel fulfilled, serving God and others being foremost. But there is also the satisfaction that comes from living as one of God's created beings. God has given to us all things to enjoy: sex, food, friends, recreation (1 Timothy 4:4; 6:17). Adult children need to receive these things gladly.

LEARN TO HANDLE FAILURE

Grown children of a friend of mine once told him, "Dad, you taught us how to succeed, but you never taught us how to fail." Sometimes we are so absorbed in succeeding that we don't look carefully at the process of failing. We need to know how to fail without being devastated by it or we won't grow. The person who is afraid to take risks is frozen in his present situation and doomed to be a slave of the past. To accept failure, we must first of all recognize that not all failure places us outside God's will. Instead, it may serve to get us back into it. Working in a seminary I see this process frequently in the lives of students. Committed to being pastors, some of them are shaken when they can't learn Greek or get interested in systematic theology. We faculty members counsel them not to despair if they choose to drop out of school to pursue another career. Learning to fail means learning through failure.

Accepting failure is also easier if we can refrain from comparing ourselves with others. Adult children stand in need of the apostle Paul's words: "When they measure themselves by themselves and compare themselves with themselves, they are not wise" (2 Corinthians 10:12). This perspective is at the core of the adult child's problem of being dependent on external cues. As our sense of self grows within us we will be less inclined to judge ourselves in the light of others. Alcoholics Anonymous wisely tells newcomers, "Identify, don't compare."

We also need to respect the challenges and complexity of problems we face. Sometimes we are beaten because the opponent is so powerful. Boston Red Sox slugger Carl Yastrzemski tells how he learned to accept this.

> The game used to eat me up. If I had a bad day it would just destroy me inside. If I went 0-for-4, I'd get so messed up, it would still affect me mentally the next day. If I went 4-for-4 I was so "up," it carried me over, too. Everything was "me." What did I do, was all that mattered. I don't know how far into my career it was—maybe 10 years—when I finally learned the secret. The thing that drives you nuts in this game is not giving credit to the other guy. Now when I go 0-for-4 I remind myself that the

pitcher had performed well, I give him the credit instead of tearing myself apart.[8]

BE MORE ASSERTIVE

Many adult children have spent their lives giving in to others. They have so little confidence in their own abilities and ideas, they let others walk all over them. Their self-esteem will grow to the degree they stop letting people push them around. One of the women in our group told us she had gone shopping for wallpaper and paint. She stepped up to the counter after finding exactly what she wanted. After looking at her selections, the clerk informed her the colors were a terrible match. "She told me she would never put them together in her home," the woman said. "Normally, this would have been devastating to me. I would have backed down, given in, and ended up going home with colors I really didn't like or want. But being in this group has boosted my self-respect so much that I surprised myself. I told the clerk that it didn't matter because I liked the colors and they were going in my home and not hers, and I bought them."

RELATE TO OTHERS

Self-esteem is not just an individual matter. We are social creatures. Self-respect grows out of being affirmed and accepted by others. We get a warm sense of being worthwhile when we are part of a group where we really feel we belong. This is why it's important to be reconciled to our own parents. God created the family as a place to belong. When we don't feel we belong there, we feel left out and lonely.

We also need to be sure that we are reconciled, when possible, to all others with whom we should be close. It helps to keep in touch with relatives and to reach out to

others around you. Adult children face some special
hindrances in relating to others. One of these is the
injured relationships they may have piled up in their
lifetime.

Two things happen to adult children in recovery that
make it important for them to seek forgiveness. First,
when they see how bizarre some of their behavior has
been, they see for the first time how they have neglected
or harmed others. They also come to realize what is true
for their parents is also true for them: Being victims does
not release them from responsibility for their actions. A
healthy, whole person does not shrink from being
accountable for what he or she has done. For this reason,
one of the twelve steps suggested by the Alcoholics
Anonymous organization for adult children states, "[We]
made a list of all persons we had harmed, and became
willing to make amends to them all." This is necessary,
they say, because we "cannot remake the present until we
undo the past."[9]

Jesus made this step crucial to our relationship to God:
"If you are offering your gift at the altar and there
remember that your brother has something against you,
leave your gift there in front of the altar. First go and be
reconciled to your brother; then come and offer your gift"
(Matthew 5:23, 24).

A few suggestions might make this resolve a bit easier.
First, give yourself time to get a more complete picture of
yourself and your family in the past. Nurture your
relationship with God so that you can draw strength from
Him to face others. Realize that any glaring unconfessed
wrong will mar your fellowship with Him. Give yourself
time to learn to forgive yourself and overcome the
perfectionism that makes it so hard to live with mistakes
and failures.

Second, when you make a list, do it thoughtfully, perhaps over a period of weeks. Because of the tendency to blame yourself needlessly, sift out the wrongs and own only the ones you have truly done.

Third, watch for less abrupt ways to spring this admission on others. Sometimes talking with them will create a context for your remarks. It will be more natural and less embarrassing for you to say, "By the way, I have something I want to clear up with you, which is. . . ."

Fourth, draw on the support of others. When you hear stories of how others have handled similar problems it will give you courage as well as know-how.

Adult children have another special obstacle in their relationships: Intimacy is difficult for them. The next chapter is devoted to making it easier.

Notes

1. David Carlson, *Counseling and Self-Esteem* (Waco, Tex.: Word, 1988), pp. 34-36.

2. Ibid., p. 36.

3. Paul W. Clement, "Self-Regulation and Self-Esteem"; "Self-Esteem: An Overview," *Your Better Self*, p. 112.

4. John D. Gartner, "Self-Esteem Tests: Assumptions and Values," *Your Better Self*, p. 99.

5. David C. Myers, "A New Look at Pride," *Your Better Self*, p. 84.

6. Roger Barrett, *Depression: What It Is and What to Do About It* (Elgin, Ill.: David C. Cook, 1977), pp. 154-55.

7. John F. Kennedy, *Profiles in Courage* cited by Donald Felker, *Building Positive Self-Concepts* (Minneapolis: Burgess Publishing, 1974), p. 35.

8. Myers, p. 92.

9. *The Twelve Steps for Adult Children*, p. 51

RESOLVE

Recognizing our struggle with intimacy we will seek to overcome our fear of it and learn how to be close to others.

10

Building Intimacy Skills

When I mentioned writing this book, a Christian woman told me, "Only recently did I learn how my mother's mental illness affected me. Because of some emotional problems I went to see a counselor. For the first time I am really dealing with my past."

"Great," I said.

"Great, yes," she replied, "But my problems have already cost me two marriages and I'm having trouble in the third."

We talked for a while about how it sometimes takes failure in our relationships to wake us up to the effect our childhood homes have had on us.

A counselor told me about a thirty-year-old woman who came for help after being divorced six times. All of her husbands had been alcoholics whom she thought she could cure. In each case, it didn't take long for the marriage to fold. He could hardly keep from laughing when she said, "I think some sort of pattern is occurring in my life." She traced this to her relationship with her alcoholic father. "I took charge of my father, doing everything I could to stop his drinking, but I failed. Apparently, I marry men in order to change them because I am unconsciously trying to do for them what I desperately tried to do for my father."

Friendships, marriage, even casual relationships can be troublesome to adult children. What they read and hear about intimacy doesn't always work for them. One woman told me how frustrated she was trying to understand her intimacy problems until she read Janet Woititz's book for adult children, *Struggle for Intimacy*. She said she had finally found someone who really understood what she was going through.

In that book Woititz explains why persons from dysfunctional families struggle with intimacy issues. First, we were set up. We had little chance to relate in the right way. "It hasn't been your fault if you have always felt that other people knew some secrets about successful relationships that you didn't know."[1]

Second, we may have felt overwhelmingly guilty because we have been so clumsy in our intimate relationships. "You are not to blame for the pain." Third, we had to make up the rules as we went along. We made mistakes and created fantasies about ideal relationships.

Travis, an ACoA, graphically describes his clumsiness and confusion over love and intimacy:

Intimate relationships are very difficult for me. I am afraid. I am also selfish at the same time. When I was young I never had the proper nurturing. Even now, I can't understand what emotional intimacy is all about. The young people I associated with were all involved in drinking, drugs, and promiscuous sex; so I was, too. I had many girlfriends and relationships, but all the relationships were based totally on sex. I do not want to de-emphasize the importance of sex in a relationship, but when that is the only basis, it is very shallow. I did not know how to share myself emotionally, so I engaged in sex. My girlfriends and I often used the term "make love" to describe our actions, but love was the one thing that was absent. I wonder why I ever told those young girls that I loved them. I wouldn't have had to tell them that to have sex with them. Sweet lies were all I was capable of. I was very afraid inside, afraid if I shared my deep feelings, I would only be hurt. I put up strong defenses to prevent my getting hurt anymore. I would hurt in order not to get hurt. The girls I lied to and abused were for my own enjoyment and that was the only way, or so I thought, that I was able to survive.

Being more intimate is an urgent matter for us moderns. Research confirms how badly we need the support that only comes from being close to people. Johns Hopkins University's health records were kept for over thirteen hundred medical students over a period of eighteen years. The persons most likely to get cancer, become mentally ill, or commit suicide, were those who had a lack of family intimacy. In another study, in Alameda, California, it was determined that those with few close contacts tended to die two to three times sooner than those who regularly shared with friends. Isolation is a high stress factor.[2] People without close affiliations even take a longer time to recover from an illness.[3]

Intimacy is one of today's most cherished values. When modern women were asked by *McCall's* magazine what they wanted most out of life, 61 percent replied, "A feeling of being close to someone." Men express the same need. When asked, "What is the ideal lover?" most replied, "Someone I can be open and honest with."

God built this need into us. When God said, "It is not good for the man to be alone," He declared we are social creatures. Being social requires attitudes and skills that are in short supply for some of us. Still, with some knowledge and patient practice, we can overcome our handicaps.

THE ART OF SELF-DISCLOSURE

Self-disclosure, the most essential element of intimacy, includes sharing your feelings, inner thoughts, needs and desires. You really don't share yourself if you exclude this inner world of feeling. No need to become psychologically naked, but you do need to be able to say "I'm angry" or "I'm sad" or "I love you" when it's appropriate to do so. This is never easy. But it may be more difficult for the adult child, whose family system was built on dishonesty.

Dishonest Dodging

Woititz claims these barriers to honesty were built because we were so occupied with dodging our family's secret, shameful problem. The addicted parent eventually stops developing emotionally. No longer does he or she make decisions and face "Sarah's" problem with math or "Jim's" trouble with the police. The chemically dependent parent acts only to maintain his habit. Lying, manipulating, and any tactic other than an honest one becomes part of the family system. Blame erupts, resentment grows, and family members become isolated strangers, each filled with various sorts of fears, despair, and anxiety, which they do not share with one another.[4]

Deliberate Distancing

Being neglected or rejected as a child can make you a distant person. In another book, I described this kind of person as the fictitious Phil: Phil felt that he loved Joyce, his wife. As a Christian he felt compelled to love his wife and felt secure in his marriage. He hadn't a jealous bone in his body. Before marrying, he had been jilted. But it didn't depress him; he never went around moping about it. He never permitted his moods to be determined by someone's feelings about him.[5]

Phil is emotionally detached; he's always been that way. His inability to love deeply is due to the fact that one or both of his parents rejected him. As a child he had to defend himself against the hurt he was constantly feeling. That defense took the form of a hard shell—an apathy toward intimacy. He convinced himself that he couldn't care less about love. Now, even when he knows he should love, he can't or won't. His indifference is like a shield of protection. People like Phil must realize that their attitude toward love is not normal and that they must learn to be able to let go and deal with their fears of intimacy.

Clearing the Way

Adult children have to search out and destroy the emotional blocks that jam their efforts to be open and honest.

Shame. We cover up because we got used to doing so. "My parents embarrassed me when I was a child; they argued in public. I would always stick up for them, even if it meant not telling the truth." We became ashamed of our feelings, thoughts, and fantasies. Our isolation from others didn't allow us to find out that others, too, had the same inner world as ours.

Fear. We are afraid of being ignored or rejected, so we project a false image. Past rejections may have hurt us so much that it is too painful to risk being ourselves. So many broken promises made us afraid to expect much, so we kept our needs and our desires to ourselves.

Unworthiness. We wonder who would really want to know us. When we think of something we could say in a conversation, we remain quiet, thinking, "Who really cares?"

Image problems. For some, particularly men, the sharing of feelings is a sign of weakness. In our culture a boy is told to keep his feelings to himself. And even if little boys do show their feelings, as men they think they've outgrown the need to do so.[6] The tough male learns to cover up. Voices from the past saying, "Don't cry, be a big boy," restrain him. If Dad was not around much or didn't talk out his feelings when he was, the son most likely will be uncomfortable showing his soft side.

Out-of-touch. "Don't feel" was the unspoken message in our homes, so we ignored our emotions. Now it may be hard to say how we feel because we don't really know how we feel.

Though it may take time, you can begin to get over these hurdles by banishing from your minds the "myths" about intimacy you may have learned in your home. Woititz lists those typical of adult child mythology.

"If you really knew me, you wouldn't care about me." In truth, care and love are built on intimacy. If a young man says to his girl, "I'm going to tell you something I've never told anyone else before," such revelations are the stuff of romance.

"If you find out I'm not perfect, you will abandon me." This fear may be real, since the child in you may feel the hurt of abandonment. But others already know you're not perfect, and they will feel closer to you when they see you are comfortable with your own imperfections. "Each of you must put off falsehood and speak truthfully to his

neighbor" (Ephesians 4:25).

"Being vulnerable always has negative results." Perhaps this has been your experience, but it's probably what you use to excuse yourself from being open. Dishonesty, not honesty, wreaks havoc with relationships. "Speaking the truth in love, we will in all things grow up into him who is the Head, that is, Christ" (Ephesians 4:15).

"You will instinctively anticipate my every need, desire, and wish." Probably a lot of nonverbal communication took place in your home; you became sensitive to the slightest changes in the problem parent so you could react in a way to keep the peace. This is unreal. Lovers and friends can't read each others' minds and always know what each other wants. We have to learn to say, "I need . . . I want. . . ."

"To be lovable, I must be happy all of the time." Adult children have this message pounded into them: "Don't cry or you will upset Daddy. Be happy or you will get Mom mad at you." Like actors, they play the right role to create the right mood, which leads to the habit of masking their true feelings.

Newlyweds may tend to start marriage this way, as did my wife Ginger. Though she had a good childhood family life, she believed a good Christian wife should be a constant source of cheer to her husband. When speaking to wives, she relates how she used to hide moments of sadness from me. These brief times of depression were times of loneliness, for she longed to share them with me but felt she shouldn't. Many months of marriage changed her mind. She tells what happened: "I soon realized how foolish my thinking was. A good wife may not always be cheerful, but she can strive to always be honest. During one of my moods, my husband asked me how I felt. `Down,' I admitted for the first time, concerned about how he would react. He surprised me by saying, `If you feel like it, here's a shoulder to cry on.' I never felt more close to him."

Christians should attempt to rejoice, but not pretend to rejoice. The notion that love obligates us to pretend in order to keep our partner happy, sober, or content is false. Love says be true to yourself and your partner, and allow him or her to be true to you.

"If I am involved with you, I will lose me." This myth, so deeply felt, dies hard. In the words of one researcher, it creates the "indifferent lover," like Pearl. She was a writer, a wife and . . . well, there wasn't time for much more. But writer is what she would underline if she were to compose her obituary. Being a wife was a high priority in her mind, but not so much in her heart. As a Christian author, she was aware of the need for loyalty to her husband, Russ. She sought to meet his needs and he didn't complain often, but he did tell her he thought she was holding something back, keeping her from being as close as he would like.

The Indifferent Lover

Pearl was in love with Russ and she was committed to him. But not without reservation. Runaway love was something impractical, something to be avoided. She had taught herself to feel this way. She had built up her defenses against love like a turtle grows a shell. She had seen too many brokenhearted girls in the college dorm, and she would not be a slave to love. She had made promises to herself as a writer. What mattered most to her was that she would have control, or, more correctly, God would have control.

She did not commit her love to Russ until she was certain he would not interfere with her goals. She wanted love, but with freedom. She felt love gave no right to one person to impose his will on another. She enjoyed her marriage for what it contributed to her, and she was willing to give in return. Sex, for example, was something she offered to her husband. She enjoyed it for the closeness. But since she had never reached a climax, she really didn't enjoy sex that much. The thrill wasn't nearly as great as having a publisher accept one of her articles.

Pearl has made herself into a "distant" partner. When she was single she learned to disengage from long relationships quickly, frequently, and without lingering pain. She knew she would have to be in charge of her emotions if she was going to be successful.[7]

Men and women like Pearl were rejected by one or both parents, just as Phil, the distant lover, was. Having been abandoned they can't hazard abandoning themselves to someone they love. One researcher claims that one-fourth of adults are either distant or indifferent lovers.

If they ever hope to change, they will need to rethink their view of priorities as well as the nature of love. They will need to see the importance of the marriage commitment, recognizing that God calls us to love with abandon.[8]

Taking Some Steps

As you rid your mind of these myths, try talking to others about your problem with intimacy. "Share your scare," a colleague of mine advises. Tell your child, your spouse, your friend that you are afraid to say how you feel. Not only does that enable them to help you, it is a very significant act of self-disclosure.

Put yourself into situations that prompt the sharing of emotions. After watching an emotional TV program with your friend or spouse, talk about how it made you feel. Walking together is great conversation starter. Talking about your dreams at breakfast is another way to feel close.

Try less threatening ways to share what's inside you. Write notes. Put a letter in your Valentine to your child or spouse. Talk into a tape recorder and give the cassette as a gift if that's easier for you.

Learn to Touch

Warm, intimate things can be said without words. Our intimacy ability will soar if we can learn to be comfortable with nonverbal intimacy. I don't mean just touching sexually, but touching sensually. Genital sexuality refers to overt forms of sexual behavior. Sensuality includes that, but also a lot more: hugging and touching to convey compassion, warmth, gentleness.

Touching doesn't have to be sexual to convey intimacy and give pleasure: a father running his hands through his nine-year-old daughter's hair; two friends celebrating good news with a gripping hug. People who make no distinction between genital sex and sensuality have a hard time being sensual without feeling sexual. Because of this a father may wrongfully stop hugging his teenage daughter, something she needs from him.

Dysfunctional family members often fail to make this distinction and it is one of the reasons they suffer from lack of intimacy. So do young, single Christian adults. Often single people have a hard time feeling close to people because they reject their sensuality along with their sexuality. Clark Barshinger, a Christian counselor, explains, "In working with college students, we have found that many Christian young adults conceive of sex genitally and therefore fail to see the relevance of their sexuality. . . . As a result they attempt to deny a very significant part of their personality which leads to repression and an unhappy compartmentalization of oneself. The end product is seeing yourself as your own worst problem and a tendency to reject your very self as too sinful to be forgiven."[9]

Through counseling and teaching, Barshinger has seen people learn to accept their sexual feelings and fantasies. They are then released to engage in more open intimacy with others on a non-genital basis. His concluding insight is powerful: "We have come to believe that it is our fear of our own sexuality that gives so much trouble in intimate relationships with others regarding the question of purity. If the sexual part of me does not have to be rejected flatly, then I am free to meet you on a more mature, holistic basis."[10]

The Clinging Lover

For some adult children, problems with intimacy will take another form. Instead of too much distance, they will require too much closeness. Janet Woititz describes the frustrating pattern of adult children who never truly bonded with their parents.

If "clingers" invest at all, they invest heavily and on a deep, emotional level. They seize the opportunity for bonding and are deeply involved before they know what is happening. In other words, they go overboard. Initially it's great. The partner is flattered, and the emotional and physical intensity feels good. The person feels energies he or she experienced in a crisis. If the partner is healthy, he will begin to feel suffocated, and the relationship drains him. He'll back off, not wanting to devote himself completely to the relationship. Ideal love evaporates as a result, and things begin to be put into perspective.

When life begins to normalize, the intensity drops and

the phone quits ringing. "Clingers" then feel rejected and let down, thinking the partner no longer cares because he no longer desires to spend every moment together. Clutching harder at the partner, they force him or her into the "I love you, go away" stance even though the partner still cares. Continuing to play out their script, they cause what they fear most: rejection and abandonment. This leaves them hurt and confused because all they wanted was a loving relationship. Thinking they picked on the wrong person, they go through the process again. Hopefully, they will realize that they have become hooked on intensity and have fooled themselves into equating that intensity with the relationship.[11]

The Anxious Lover

In marriage, clingers are "anxious lovers." After seven years, marriage was good for Joyce, but not secure. Yet it wasn't for lack of love for Phil. Usually, she was obsessed by him: clinging to him when together, dreaming of him when apart. Around other women, she felt jealous of him; when he was gone, she was anxious, wondering what he was up to. Her feelings fluctuated often, zooming to new heights when she was in his arms, plunging to the cellar whenever he was distant and indifferent to her.

Phil complained of Joyce smothering him, and became frustrated over always trying to prove he loved her. To him she was an emotional extortioner, demanding affection and never getting enough. Phil was confused about Joyce's bottomless emotional pit and very tired of trying to fill it up with affection.[12]

Anxious, clinging lovers will do well to see the source of their problem. For Joyce, love is an obsession that makes her extremely possessive and often jealous. She simply can't trust. Her emotions are too tied to her husband's reactions to her.   Anxious lovers report that one parent was coolly demanding and distant. Women had love from their mothers, but indifference and hostility from their fathers. For men it was the other way around. Dad was involved with them, but Mom wasn't. Rejected in childhood, they are starving for someone to truly love them. Some intensely fear they will die if abandoned.

Not only rejection, but co-dependence can create this clinging tendency. Never having developed a sense of self, the abuser's or addict's child has a fused personality. If, before marriage, such a person doesn't properly differentiate as I described in chapter 7, he or she will fuse with someone else. The unfused person simply relates to the married partner in the same way he or she related to the problem parent. This explains why a daughter of an alcoholic might fall in love with one. She mistakes caring for loving because her family did.

Her alcoholic partner needed someone who would care; she needed someone to care for. So she married him to fix him. As long as she can concentrate on his problem, she need not face her own. Instead of a healthy union, they have created a morbid fusion. As long as he depends on her to solve his problem he won't tackle it himself, just as she won't solve her own problems because she's trying to solve his. He doesn't grow, she doesn't grow. Hand in hand they slide down the inevitable alcoholic slope toward disaster. Her enormous passion to be needed, which she mistakes as love, makes her deaf to saner voices that say, "Stop protecting your husband. Let him face his own problem." Though he lashes out at her, even beats her, she will still cling because it's what she's used to, what she's comfortable with. Insecurity is her security.[13]

Freedom to Love

Freeing oneself from a fused relationship doesn't always require physical separation, though that might be wise where there is danger to a spouse or children. Breaking free does demand an emotional separation. All I have written in this book applies to this process. Handling this separateness in marriage can best be described by the following statements.

You can be you:

I love you as you are. I don't use love as a weapon to get you to change.

I accept you.

I allow you to be different.

I don't criticize or nag, but give you honest feedback.

I allow you to have your interests.

I give you time.

I am not jealous of your successes.

I can be me:

I don't feel I have to do everything with you.

I don't feel I must make you happy all of the time.

I don't have to react to your feelings unnecessarily.

I differentiate between what is our concern and what is mine, and I don't drag you in.

You are not jealous of my successes.

I can assert myself without feeling guilty or disloyal to you.

Yet, we are one:

We enjoy fully our romantic and sexual closeness.

We play together.

We share equally life's responsibilities.

We create together.

We go through crises hand in hand.

We spend time with God together.

We talk about our differences and try to resolve our conflicts.

We freely express our feelings and support one another emotionally.

We serve others and God as partners.

MARRIAGE MATTERS

After attending a lecture on the alcoholic family, a man told of how much light it shed on his marriage.

My father-in-law is an alcoholic. My wife's family has been the source of a lot of marital stress. I get upset because she spends so much time worrying about them or trying to help them. Visits to their home are always troubling, not merely because of the difficulty of relating to them or seeing my father-in-law drunk, but of seeing the stress this puts on my wife. After this lecture, I can trace other marital problems to my wife's alcoholic family. My wife needs help in learning how to deal properly with her family and what it has done to her.

This man's experiences are so typical. He married an adult child, ready to face occasional embarrassment over his father-in-law's drinking. But he was not prepared for the other complications. If married adult children can be alert to these potential marital tensions, they can be in a good position to deal with them.

Special Traits, Special Troubles

After learning of the possible traits of the adult child, a little imagination will tell you how each of them might affect a marriage. Not all of the impact is bad. Many adult children may be loyal to a fault, and often they make devoted marriage partners. "Pleasers" are usually sensitive, considerate partners.

Of one of them, a wife said, "My husband may not be the happiest person, but it's hard to find one who is more kind."

On the other hand, the tendency for an adult child to be depressed and guilt-ridden will burden the partner. You may be so unsure about what to do in situations that your mate gets frustrated while you are struggling to make up your mind. Or else you may hurt your spouse as one woman says she does:

I was born out of wedlock and my mother married two abusive alcoholics. We moved around constantly, never in the same house more than a year or so. I have no sentimental traditions. I don't remember other people's birthdays because these weren't important in my childhood. This has been a source of friction now, between my husband (who has strong family traditions) and myself. I often intentionally trivialize the things he does out of tradition or sentimentality.

You may also be uptight about whether or not you are doing the right thing. Your partner tells you to relax and not take everything so seriously. Yet you strive to do things that make you feel good about yourself because doing the wrong thing makes you feel so guilty. Your partner may not understand why you do what you do because he or she can't see the reason that lies in the past. A husband reveals, "Much of my `good' feeling today comes from doing the opposite of what occurred in my childhood home."

Obviously, as you improve yourself, you will improve your marriage. In the meantime, it will help a lot if you can admit your shortcomings and, along with your spouse, explore how they have put a strain on your relationship. Your partner can be your most valuable ally in your battle to break the cycle.

In-law Relationships

Suppose an adult child, still trapped in a co-dependent relationship with her childhood family, marries someone who properly detached from his own family. When his normalcy clashes with his partner's abnormalcy, look out. Things can get quite distressful and confusing.

For starters, there's the outsider syndrome. The dysfunctional family may consciously inflict the in-law with alien status. Not only might they attack him because he's different, but because he's a threat to their system.

Sometimes the in-law feels like an outsider simply because the family system looks so foreign. The outsider's feeling starts with visits to the home, which are strangely uncomfortable. It can get far more serious if the outsider starts tampering with the in-law's family. Pointing a finger at the secret family problem may turn him into the new family scapegoat who takes on the blame for their condition.

Most problems will revolve around relating to the adult child who is still unhealthily attached to her family. Issues can be painfully personal. It will hurt to see your spouse, an adult child, revert to being a child again whenever she is around her parents. Issues can be quite earthy, like financial ones. The alcoholic family may be in a financial crisis. How much should you help? Saying no to an alcoholic father-in-law's pleas for money might be easy, but refusing to go along with your wife signing over a check to him may be terribly difficult.

Problems can be daily ones, like regular phone calls which bring bad news and complaint from your spouse's family, keeping her depressed and afraid. Other problems may put you in a bind. Do you let your mother-in-law babysit your children? If your father-in-law is abusive, do you consent to your kid spending a weekend with him? Thankfully, there are ways of coping with these problems.

First, you will need to avoid being sucked into your spouse's family system. You must shun the urge to solve their problems for them. Respect your in-laws' right to continue in their problem, just as you respect your right to refuse to solve it for them. You must also resist the urge to fight them; remember the co-dependent is as much enslaved by rebellion as she is by conformity. If you aren't drawn into their problem as a sympathetic lamb to the slaughter, you will be inclined to be like a lion and attack them for their shortcomings. Rather, you must try to be legitimately involved with them while insisting on the emotional, functional, and economic independence of the two families.

Be honest with them. If you don't want your child to stay overnight with his grandparents because of the grandfather's drinking, tell them the truth. Give no place to denial, manipulation, overconcern, repression, and disillusional thinking, typical of dysfunctional families. Show your love and respect in other ways. Arrange for grandparents to see your child even if you won't let him stay overnight with them. Don't punish or hurt them by withholding what is due them. Resist cutting off all ties just because they don't know how to draw proper boundaries.

Not only will you need to shun being co-dependent with your spouse's family, you will have to resist becoming a co-dependent with your spouse. In other words, if your spouse is riding the roller coaster with her parents, you must be sure you don't ride it with her.

Your first response will be to jerk your spouse out of the snare. But then you are doing exactly what your spouse is doing. She's trying to save her family just like you are trying to save her from saving her family. The only way out is to refuse to protect your spouse in unhealthy ways and refuse to cooperate in any improper ways of protecting her family. To do this, you may need the support of a group like Alanon, just as your spouse needs it. Both of you must aim to properly relate to the troubled parents without allowing your own marriage and family to become hopelessly tangled up with them.

If you are the co-dependent, you need to follow suggestions like the ones I've given in chapter 7. Your major task is to properly extract yourself from your family's trap. If your family has scapegoated or rejected your spouse, you are in a terrible bind. Your family insists that loyalty to your spouse amounts to betraying them. The pressure on you can be oppressive.

The dysfunctional family of a woman I know bombarded her husband with criticism and rejection. Bewildered, he tried but was unable to keep peace with her family. To maintain his own sanity, he visited them less often, drawing more complaints from them. The parents attacked the husband, insisting their daughter see how abnormal he was. She talked to me about how she was asked to take a stand between her parents and her husband. Without hesitation I told her to side with her husband. Scripture is clear that loyalty to one's spouse comes before loyalty to one's parents (Genesis 2:24). She eventually was forced to do what many adult children must: break with her family for the sake of her marriage. A co-dependent will no doubt need the support of a counselor or support group to take such a drastic measure.

SEX MATTERS

In my experience counseling adult children, I have observed that a significant percentage of them have serious problems related to sex. Because people block out of their memory traumas like an incestuous experience, they often fail to see how the past is the cause of their present disorder. Yet sex therapist Mary Ann Mayo and others are emphatic about the role of childhood background in such problems as inability to relax during sex, aversion to sexual advances, inhibited orgasm, etc.[14] Problems can show up in the areas of sexual desire as well as sexual functioning.

Low Sexual Desire

Identifying low sexual desire isn't easy since there are no clear guidelines about how much or how often a person should want sex. Some people have no desire whatsoever, submitting to their partner as a chore. Others enjoy sex once in a while but not often. Symptoms of a problem exist if your mate complains of needing sex a lot more than you do. No one can tell you how much sex is enough. According to Scripture, enough is when your mate is kept from undue temptation to lust after others (1 Corinthians 7:1-7) and when your sex life contributes to the love and intimacy between you.

As a guide for measuring your sexual desire, you might consider that couples usually report having sex two or three times a week. If you are under forty-five years of age and want sex less than once every two weeks, or over forty-five and desire it less than once a month, you ought to consider seeing a sex therapist.[15]

Normally, people with low sexual desire have sexual feelings, but they have unconsciously shut them off. They do it with internal thoughts: "I'm no good. I'm not attractive. I can't last long enough to satisfy her."[16]

Self-blaming adult children may inhibit their sexual desire by guilt or hostility, which spills over into this area. A man may reject women because, deep down, he harbors resentment toward them. Or a woman may feel angry toward her husband because she was abandoned by her father.

Sex therapists talk about those with "The Madonna-Prostitution Complex" who can have sex with "bad" people but not "good" ones. Associating sex with power, they are turned on by a partner who is "inferior" to themselves. Afraid of true intimacy, they cannot trust their spouse in a close relationship, such as a sexual one. Any kind of abandonment or abuse, especially incest, can produce this attitude. In incest situations, the child usually cannot even trust the other parent. With no one to turn to, the adult child learns not to trust. In the words of one expert, as a child he or she had no "safe harbor."

Incest sometimes made the child feel powerful, as when a father rewarded his daughter with privileges or gifts, or made her feel special because of their sexual relationship. In the process, the child failed to learn other forms of intimacy, and tied sex to power instead of closeness.

This may account for the numerous persons I have counseled who had little or no desire for sex after marriage even though they had enjoyed it before. Prior to marriage, when sex to them was illegitimate, it turned them on because they equated sex with something bad. Once married, sex lost its passion because it lost its badness. Or else, equating sex with power, their desire to win their mates made them passionate. After marriage, they lost the need for sex because they no longer had the need to control. Their mates may accuse them of consciously deceiving and manipulating them.

262   Part Two: Resolving the Past

Actually, their passion before marriage was genuine. The passion vanished because the purpose for it did. They may not want sex much because they are now getting power in other ways. As overachievers, workaholics substitute the activities of the board room for those of the bedroom. Even "clingers" can have low sexual desire. Unable to enjoy a truly close physical relationship, they may demand their spouse spend inordinate amounts of time with them to overcome their lack of a truly close physical relationship. Knowing their mate is less than happy with their sex life may make the anxious lover more jealous and suspicious.

Extreme Sex Desire

Sex is such an obsession for some people that the term *sexual addiction* is applied to them. Persons who want to make love to their spouses a lot aren't necessarily sexually addicted, even though their partner may think they are. Being obsessed with sex is not just a matter of how often a person wants to have sex, but a matter of how and with whom. Sex addicts constantly fantasize about sex, masturbate frequently in any given day, and usually become hooked on pornographic material. If a man is married, he may neglect sex with his wife in preference for masturbation, because sex addicts dread true intimacy.

Some adult children developed the traits of sexual addiction during their childhoods. They may have coped with a stressful family situation by withdrawing and using the pleasures of solitary sex as a way to deal with their unhappiness. Or else they learned to associate sex with power, concentrating on pornography that portrays sex in this way. Sex became a substitute for the legitimate forms of intimacy missing from their lives.

Sexual Functioning

A wife might have severe pain during intercourse or be unable to have an orgasm. A husband may be unable to have an erection or sustain one for very long, or he may be unable to ejaculate or may ejaculate too soon.

Scores of reasons can contribute to these difficulties, not all of them connected to a dysfunctional family background. But being an adult child could contribute to any of them. Severe guilt, anger, or other emotions typical of adult children can cause functional problems. Deep-down guilt may keep a man from having an erection and enjoying sex. If guilt and/or shame is driving the man to overachieve, it may make him feel that marriage and sex get in the way. Though he tries to respond to his wife's needs, his body won't. In this case, his problem with sex depends on his dealing with his problem of overachieving, which requires his dealing with his problem with his parents.

A woman whose body becomes so rigid that she can't have intercourse without pain may be suffering from a lack of trust, which is no doubt linked to the kind of relationship she had with her father. One who beat, frightened, or severely criticized his daughter may have destroyed what faith she might have had in men. A father who was never emotionally close, was gone most of the time, or showed little interest in her didn't build her confidence in men. Studies show that women who are non-orgasmic did not receive the kind of affirmation and protection from their fathers to develop inside them the kind of trust that permits intimate surrender to a man, which is what orgasm in sexual intercourse represents.[17] They become distant lovers, afraid to let go, emotionally and sexually.

Treat Yourself

Sexual problems are treatable. Start with a medical check-up to be sure something is not wrong physically.

If things are okay physically, then do some reading about your problem. Besides teaching you a lot, good literature can help you develop a positive attitude toward sex. *The Gift of Sex*, written by a Christian couple, will help you think rightly about sex in marriage, as well as provide do-it-yourself sex therapy, describing clearly tested techniques for treating various common problems. Consult other books for more specific problems. For example, women who have difficulty being orgasmic would benefit from reading *For Yourself: The Fulfillment of Female Sexuality*.[18]   *Out of the Shadows* deals frankly with sexual addiction.[19]

Continuing your recovery as an adult child will definitely help you with your sex life.   Almost always, our problems with sex are problems of the personality. Sex is tied into our capacity to live, to be intimate, to give, to receive, to lose ourselves in another. For example, if control is an issue with us in general, it will be an issue in sex. Who is in control is a major item in the game of making love. A woman who is insecure when she isn't managing things may get uptight over her husband's sexual advances because they signal he is trying to control her. Because of this, it's wise for a husband to permit his wife to take charge of the lovemaking if she has rape, incest, or other damaging sexual experiences in her background.

If your problem has gone on for months, or as a couple you aren't working well together at solving it, consult a counselor. While any counselor can help, you may want to go to one who specializes in sex therapy. With special help you might overcome your problem in a few weeks, or at least make marked improvement.

The treatment for severe sexual addiction is similar to treatment for other addictions, which includes help from a counselor and support groups. Control of inappropriate sex is coupled with learning to enjoy marital sex for intimacy and companionship and not just for excitement. It may take years for couples to shed wrong attitudes toward sex that they took with them on their honeymoon. As they mature as individuals and as a couple, sex will become less associated with power, guilt, badness, hurt, and fear, and will be identified with closeness and unselfish, sacrificial giving of each to the other. The remedy for wrong sex or little sex is cultivating a close, satisfying sensual relationship within the bonds of marriage.

THE INTIMATE ADVENTURE

I once heard the popular family specialist Charlie Shedd say, "I view my wife as a forest and myself as an explorer." Getting close to someone can be one of life's most exciting adventures. Yet, just as in other exploration of new territory, there is an element of danger in intimacy. "Intimacy is always difficult," claims one expert, "and when it stops being difficult, it stops being intimacy."[20] Getting closer to others will demand some risktaking. You'll probably never know people the way you would like to or be completely comfortable being yourself, but you can keep working on it. No need to always take big risks. Try risking just one degree above your comfort zone. As you get rewarding results, you'll break out of your shell and into others', bit by bit.

Notes

1. Janet Woititz, *Struggle for Intimacy* (Pompano Beach, Fla.: Health Communications, 1985), p. 1.

2. William Hulme, *Managing Stress in Ministry* (San Francisco: Harper & Row, 1985).

3. Benjamin Gottlieb, ed., *Social Networks and Social Support in Community Mental Health*, N.Y.: Sage Publications, 1981), p. 16.

4. Woititz, *Adult Children of Alcoholics*.

5. Charles Sell, *House on the Rock*, (Wheaton, Ill.: Victor Books, 1987) p. 66.

6. Osherson, pp. 6-8.

7. Daniel Goleman, "Heart of Cupid: Love Ills, Thrills Tied to Childhood," *Arizona Republic*, 22 September 1985, sec. AA, p. 11.

8. Sell, *House on the Rock*, pp. 66-69.

9. Eugene Clark Barshinger, "Living the Single Life: On Singleness, Intimacy and Maturity," paper presented to the Wheaton Bible Church Career Group Retreat, January 1976, p. 16.

10. Ibid., p. 8

11. Woititz, *Struggle for Intimacy*, p. 31.

12. Sell, *House on the Rock*, pp. 65-66.

13. Fossum and Mason, pp. 144-45.

14. Mary Ann Mayo, *A Christian Guide to Sexual Counseling* (Grand Rapids, Mich.: Zondervan, 1987), pp.114-15.

15. Ibid., p. 140.

16. Ibid., p. 141.

17. Ibid., pp. 154-55.

18. Lonnie Barbach, *For Yourself: The Fulfillment of Female Sexuality* (New York: Anchor, 1976).

19. Patrick Carnes, *Out of the Shadows* (Minneapolis: CompCare Publications, 1983).

20. Andrew Greeley, *Sexual Intimacy* (Chicago: The Thomas More Press), p. 26.

Finished Business?

Working on unfinished business may be a lifetime project for some adult children. Sensing the depth of the past's impact, they seem to recognize that recovery is a process, not a certain goal. They are uneasy about claiming they have really gotten past the past. Paul was that way when I asked him the other day if he could say he has recovered.

I'm kind of afraid to say that. If I do, something will happen tomorrow that will make me feel like I'm not. I would say I have recovered substantially. I still have a general fear of failure. If my expectation is to be fully recovered and I don't achieve it, then I'll feel guilty that I've not done something I should have.

Like captives long hostage to our problems, we find it hard to believe we're free even if we might be.

Then, too, some of our habits are so deep-seated. Recently I was talking to my wife about my efforts to stop my impulse to criticize most everything she says. Two hours later she made a perfectly good suggestion which I promptly censored.   Detecting what I had just done, I apologized: "Sorry, I did it again."   At least I've improved a bit: I now catch myself after I've said the wrong thing; stopping myself before I blurt it out is tough.

As Christians, we can accept this, knowing there is always more to change. Life is dynamic. Perfection comes only in eternity: We shall finally be like Christ when we see Him as He is (1 John 3:2).

Yet adult children who practice the resolves of *Unfinished Business* do experience some liberating victories in their battles with the past. To share some of these with you and sum up this book, I interviewed Paul and Kurt, who have been in recovery since they first met with me in my office two years ago.   Though their journeys are distinct, they are somewhat alike. Drawing upon their stories and others, I can illustrate a few of the high points of the recovery process.

AWARENESS AVENUES

Both Kurt and Paul admitted there would be no recovery without awareness of what the past had done to them. Paul, who is thirty-eight years old, said:

I didn't like myself. There was always a general uneasiness, a dissatisfaction inside. I was never good enough and I felt that I never would be. When I read an article about ACoAs, which was probably a short review of Woititz's book, Adult Children of Alcoholics I saw myself and my siblings in the description. A light went on and there was a reason why I felt the way I did. Seeing that there was a cause meant to me that I could change things. If there was a cause, I could reverse it; that was in itself healing. A great burden was lifted by this initial awareness which gave me hope.

How I thought and felt about myself as an adult had roots in my childhood experience. There was no way I could get beyond the limitations imposed by those feelings, thoughts, and relationship patterns without going back to discover how they got into place and where they came from. How had my environment caused me to feel and behave the way I did? In order to make changes, I had to go back and get an understanding of what happened.

Kurt:

When you spoke in class about your own background was the first moment I suspected my personal problems might be related to mine. Then, when I read the list that was handed out in class describing characteristics of adult children, I finally knew the source of my struggles with drugs, a lousy self-image, and lots of other things. The healing began then.

Yet both men agreed there was something besides awareness that got them started.

PERMISSION POINT

Paul said he needed permission:

It was hard to accept what the ACoA article said even though it graphically described my life. I couldn't accept the idea that the past was what made me like I was. As a Christian, I guess I thought I was beyond the past's influence. I thought my problems were merely caused by my personal sin and failure to obey God. However, when you told me about your struggles, I felt free to accept the fact that mine might also be due to the past. You gave me permission to look into it.

Saying much the same thing, Kurt put it in other words:

You gave me the courage to link my personal problems to my past. Until then, I always felt my problems were just sinful acts and that I had to measure up. Then, when you talked about yourself in class, it was the first time I ever heard a Christian leader speak about how an alcoholic family background had affected him. I said to myself, "Maybe my changing isn't just a matter of trying harder not to sin. Maybe I have some hang-ups I need to work on." The ball started rolling then. It took a year to work on the denial and then things began to happen.

PAINFUL PATHS

Adult children typically tell of the hurt they feel when they revisit their pasts.

Kurt: "After overcoming my denial, things got worse. When it (my past with its problems) came out, and it came out strong, sometimes I would literally shake and I would have nightmares."

Terri, a student in my class on alcoholism and the family, wrote a journal as she worked through her injurious childhood. She tells of her struggle to get beyond the pain:

More than once I have had to say to myself, "Terri, get hold of yourself." More often, it seems, came the times when I felt unlovable, depressed and all alone. I didn't want to write down my thoughts because they were haunting all my waking moments already. I didn't want to get more depressed than I already was. I would go to counseling and cry or be furiously angry. I would read a book or attend alcoholism class and nearly fall apart from all the stimuli triggering memories of my horrid past. I would try to communicate with my fiancé and then decide I was not worthy of his love. (I decided I wasn't a person of worth, period.) It was bad enough that I couldn't sleep at night; why should I force myself to write it all down?

Yet adult children know the meaning of the statement,

"The truth shall make you free, but first it may make you miserable." Wrote Terri:

So there were the times when I read several good books and learned to detach and love myself. In class and counseling I allowed myself to feel and resolve major levels of anger. I read my Bible, prayed, and wrote in my journal with ease. But it was during the times when I couldn't move, when my strength was sapped, that I learned the most.

ACCEPTANCE ACRES

Dealing with unfinished business requires the support of others. Paul was emphatic about this point:

What helped me the most was just talking and thinking out loud with the counselor. It was an accepting relationship. I could just sit there with someone who was not going to judge me, criticize, or reject me for what I was saying and thinking. Then, I found support and acceptance in the ACoA group where there were people who understood me. My wife was also very understanding.

This helped me to begin accepting myself exactly the way I was at that point in time. It's a frightening thing to let your defenses down and be faced with yourself for the first time in your life. It was a scary process. While going through this process I had to have others' support and acceptance; I could not have done it alone.

For Kurt the group was a safe spot to air out things that were troubling him inside:

The group gave me a place where I could acknowledge in a Christian environment that I was really angry and then bring up all the issues I had been facing. I could reveal things that came up that I was ashamed of, like my desire

*to date younger girls. When I began dealing with my
past, I found myself wondering what it was like to date
and be accepted by a nice fifteen-year-old girl, since all
my dates in my teen years were with very troubled girls.
Here I was, a twenty-eight-year-old man, wondering that
out loud to the group without anyone jumping on me for
it.*

Apparently many adult children don't find this kind
of acceptance in their day-to-day lives. "I'm scared of
church groups," admitted Kurt. "ACoA groups I have no
problem with." I asked Paul, who had been a dedicated
Christian for twenty years why he hadn't found such
acceptance in the churches he attended. His answer:

*I don't know for sure. Perhaps it was my fault. I don't
feel I was ever in a relationship where my defenses
weren't up. I needed others' acceptance so much that I
couldn't relate to them honestly. I felt I must do things to
please them so that they would like me. I just couldn't
bring myself to give them a good look at who I really was.*

*Yet perhaps it wasn't all me. I can remember feeling that
the church we were attending before coming here expected
an awful lot: a problem-free Christian life. I don't know if
it was my particular sensitivities or if it was just that you
weren't supposed to have any problems; there was
something drastically wrong with you if you did.*

EMOTIONAL ELEVATIONS

Emotional changes are sometimes spectacular.
Personally, after dealing with the issues for the past two
years, at fifty-five years of age I feel happier than I can
remember. Much more content, I don't worry like I did
just a few years ago. Guilt doesn't always plague me; I
can relax and enjoy life as never before.

Paul's emotional change was dramatic:

Depression was what forced me into counseling: I was unable to function at all when I sought help. The depression is gone, along with the pervading sense of sadness that I always had.

I have also become emotionally self-aware. Now I can sense when I'm angry, sad, or scared about something, and can figure out where it came from and what I can do about it. If it means sharing it with someone, I can do that. It's like I'm no longer a victim of emotions that I can't understand. I am in touch with them and can resolve them and get back at peace with myself.

I can also be more intimate, more honest with people. I now realize how emotionally isolated I was from people, even though I was interacting with others every day.

ROUGH ROADS

As far as I know, each of our group members has emotions and behaviors that are especially slow to change. Intimacy is still a major problem for Kurt:

I can't seem to get close to people, particularly to girls. My relationships with them go in cycles. I get a bit close and then something happens to end the relationship. No opposite-sex friends; that's my greatest problem. Right now I am at the point where I have almost given up. I don't know what the problem is. That's why I am thinking about getting back into the group so that I can meet people and warm up. After a certain point, it's difficult.

"I still get angry," said Paul, "especially if I sense people controlling and manipulating me, expecting me to be what they want instead of allowing me to be who I am."

Only recently alert to one of his trouble spots, Paul is hopeful of some exciting breakthroughs. "I've not achieved intimacy with God as much as I have with others. This is something I just realized. I have learned how to trust and get close to others, now I need to do the same with Him. Not relating so much to Him intellectually, but relating to Him emotionally; letting Him get near to who I am and where I hurt. I still tend to feel like I've got to have it all together first before I talk to Him."

SELF-RESPECT SUMMIT

Because lack of self-respect is the core issue with most adult children, a new sense of self is a high point on every adult child's map of recovery.

Self-confidence is what Kurt was gaining:

I used to get headaches all the time because everything I felt, everything I did was wrong. Dr. Kantzer said in class that some in this room were going to be liberal; I just knew it would be me—that sort of thing. Whenever anything was wrong, I was always the first to admit it. That has changed. I've felt really good about myself in the past year.

Kurt's problem was due to his external orientation; he was always wanting to prove himself to others. "If I did not produce as well as others, that was not good. I was a failure. I was not producing and I should be producing, and somehow there was a fault there. Now I am more confident about who I am without comparing myself with others all the time."

Paul placed enormous stress on the role his new sense of self played in the progress he'd made:

Becoming aware of who we are and accepting that . . . that's recovery. What stands out to me at this point, looking back to when I began the recovery process and where I am now, is that I have a much more firmly

*established sense of my own identity than I ever had
before. I think I spent many years trying to form my
identity, self-concept, and self-esteem based on my living
up to other people's expectations. In order to feel good
about myself I thought I had to earn the approval and
acceptance of other people based on what I did. That
certainly began when I tried to please my dad when I was
a kid. Yet I never really felt I had pleased him well
enough. This carried into my adult life. I was finally
able to see that it wasn't working. I was doing all I could
to please people, but I didn't know who I was on the
inside.*

*I feel at peace—much more relaxed, much less anxious,
and more comfortable with myself. I am not so afraid I
am going to meet someone today, sense that I haven't
pleased them, and feel my self-esteem plunge downward.*

Paul's self-acceptance makes him eager to continue to
discover himself:

*I feel as though my motivation has moved from external
to internal. I am now motivated by finding out what all
is inside of me: what strengths God has put there; what I
can do; how much further I can grow as an individual;
how much more I can learn about myself as God's
creation. Living up to other people's expectations was so
limiting to me as a person, covering up whatever was
unique to me with those external expectations. The lid
has been lifted off. Now I'm discovering who I am and
I'm feeling secure enough to accept what I find, which is a
real big difference from the insecurity I had about myself
over the years.*

This emphasis on self-discovery raises a question that I
put to Paul. "Isn't this stress on expressing yourself
instead of pleasing others a form of selfishness?" His
answer showed he had thought about and resolved this
issue.

My past relationships were self-centered. I was in relationships with people for what I needed from them, in terms of an identity. At this point, I can accept the fact that God accepts me just the way I am and I can be secure in that and begin to relate to people in terms of what I can give of myself to them. It's a different orientation altogether. Not that I am trying to meet my own needs or secure my identity or self-worth. Now I can accept the fact that God gives me those things and that He has created me as a unique person. He accepts me and I can accept myself and give all that I am as an individual to other people.

Though Kurt and Paul each have more self-respect, they stress different ways of gaining it.

Kurt's own self-acceptance is due in large part to the new acceptance he has from others. Also, he feels better about himself through attempts to do things.

I was sort of stifled in any attempt I made to artistically express myself. Now I am taking ballet lessons. The other day I had a chance to show off a bit. At the health club there was a group of high school girls practicing some ballet routines. I showed them I could do them; they were impressed. My teacher is a very positive person, too. During our lessons she has us look into the mirror and smile at ourselves. She gives us a hug whenever we leave. This is all part of my recovery.

Initially, Paul said that the acceptance of others was what helped him the most. Now, he believes it is the acceptance he feels from God that is the biggest part of his new sense of self.

I am really beginning to feel experientially that God does accept me and that He loves me and that is enough. I can be secure enough to reach out to other people, giving my real self to them, and not feel I must use a false self to take from them to meet my own needs.

Even though I became a Christian years ago and knew that I was saved, I still based my relationship to God on how well I measured up. At this point I am secure in feeling that God accepts me. This has come through a continual process of understanding and accepting myself in the context of feeling the acceptance of others. God has mediated His acceptance through the unconditional care and concern of other Christians.

HIGHER-POWER PEAK

From a Christian viewpoint, no map of recovery would be complete if it didn't point to God. From Him we receive identity and life. "For in him we live and move and have our being" (Acts 17:28). In His Son, Jesus Christ, we receive freedom from all guilt, for He died for all our sins: past, present, and future. Helpless to save ourselves, we trust in His salvation, not our own good works: "For it is by grace you have been saved, through faith . . . not by works, so that no one can boast. For we are God's workmanship, created in Christ Jesus to do good works, which God prepared in advance for us . . . " (Ephesians 2:8-10).

His power sustains us in our recovery, as Terri relates:

Writing in my journal was difficult. It was hard to be consistent. It was hard to feel. It was hard to process through memories. There were times of great insight when God seemed to speak so clearly to me. He would help me to recognize and battle against self-defeating behaviors, such as dwelling on negative thoughts and wallowing in self-pity. He would use anything He could—books, sermons, hymns, Scripture, people—to comfort me or kick me in the seat of my pants. One Wednesday, January 18, I wrote, "I have felt the power and victory of self-control and prayers. I have poured out my heart to God and I believe He has heard me and continues to hear me. In times of depression that seem so deep, I find peace from prayer—slowing down physically and mentally and relaxing, not dwelling on bad things, reading and meditating on Bible verses."

Most of all, we bask in God's love for us. Terri continues:

I am able to love myself not because of what I've done to deal with my past and bring healing—though being counseled, writing a journal, and reading books are all admirable things—but because God counts me worthy of His love.

> *Jesus loves me, this I know,*
> *for the Bible tells me so.*
> *Little ones to him belong,*
> *they are weak, but He is strong.*

The words of this simple song brought alive to me the truth of God's love for me, and so I love myself.

I can think of no more appropriate words to end this book. Thanks, Terri, for reminding us of what we need most to resolve our unfinished business.

Appendix

For help in starting or locating support groups, contact ADULT CHILDREN OF ALCOHOLICS, P.O. Box 140175, Chicago, IL 60614-0175, Phone: (312) 929-4581. The following are Christian organizations which sponsor groups for addicted persons and family members, including adult children.

OVERCOMERS OUTREACH
2290 W. Whittier Blvd., Suite D
La Habra, CA 90631
Phone: (213) 697-3994

AL-ANON FAMILY GROUP HEADQUARTERS
1372 Broadway (at 38th Street)
7th Floor
New York, NY 10018
Phone: (800) 245-4656

ADULTS MOLESTED AS CHILDREN UNITED
c/o Parents United
P.O. Box 952
San Jose, CA 95108
Phone: (408) 280-5055

INCEST SURVIVORS ANONYMOUS
P.O. Box 5613
Long Beach, CA 90805-0613
Phone: (213) 428-5599

OVEREATERS ANONYMOUS
World Service Office
4025 Spencer St.
Torrance, CA 90503
Phone: (213) 542-8363